THE FREE CHURCH

A Treatise on Church Polity with Special Relevance
To Doctrine and Practice in Christian
Churches and Churches of Christ

By

James DeForest Murch

RESTORATION PRESS

AUTHOR'S PREFACE

This book is a polemic written to strengthen the faith of Disciples of Christ in the form of church polity to which they have been committed for more than 150 years.

Disciples are congregationalists (with a small "c") because they believe that the completely autonomous local church is the church after the New Testament pattern.

Strangely enough (probably because everyone took the Free Church ideal as a matter of course) only one definitive work on the subject has been produced by our people: *Church Polity* by W. L. Hayden (1894), long out of print.[1] There has been a growing need for a scholarly work on the subject which would be relevant to the modern church situation, especially in view of the plan to "Restructure the Brotherhood." While I was pondering the possibility of writing such a volume the following incident occurred:

One day while Mrs. Murch and I were attending the 1965 World Convention of Churches of Christ in San Juan, Puerto Rico, I met

Darrell K. Wolfe, director of the Bethany Press, in the lobby of the San Jeronimo Hilton Hotel. We fell to discussing Brotherhood affairs, and I casually expressed concern that while the Bethany Press had published many volumes in favor of Restructure, they had issued nothing against it. Mr. Wolfe assured me that this was not due to any bias, but simply because they had received no manuscripts of real quality presenting the opposing view. When I intimated that I was contemplating this book, *The Free Church*, he immediately expressed an interest in it and asked if I could prepare a rather detailed Synopsis of the work for consideration by his Book Committee. Upon my return to Washington, I sent the Synopsis, but Bethany Press advised me that, because of previous commitments and a tight publication schedule, it was unable to promise publication. In his cordial letter[2] notifying me of the situation, Mr. Wolfe said, "I believe that your manuscript ought to be published without delay."

Since the news of my project had got around, almost immediately one of our fine Christian foundations offered to underwrite publication. This volume is the result.

I am deeply indebted to many sources for the information which the book contains. The Notes and Bibliography appended acknowledge some of these. Among the individuals who have given advice, criticism and/or encouragement in various ways are John Bolten, Robert W. Burns, Malcom K. Burton, Rolland L. Ehrman, Henry David Gray, B. D. Phillips, Claude E. Spencer, Dean E. Walker, and Darrell K. Wolfe. To all, my profound appreciation.

Possibly, after "the tumult and the shouting" of the Restructure controversy "die," I may revise the book for use as an objective, definitive, scholarly text in our church schools and seminaries. Meanwhile, I pray that it may be used as an effective and convincing polemic for the preservation and perpetuation of the Free Church way of life among the great Brotherhood of Christian Churches and Churches of Christ.

JAMES DeFOREST MURCH

Washington, D. C.

CONTENTS

Chapter   *Page*

	Author's Preface	v
I.	Freedom in Christ	1
II.	The New Testament Church	12
III.	The Rise of Catholicism	25
IV.	The Free Church Tradition	36
V.	The Choice on the Frontier	49
VI.	Individual Freedom	60
VII.	Congregational Freedom	70
VIII.	Ministerial Freedom	79
IX.	Freedom of Association	90
X.	Corporative Co-operation	100
XI.	Restructure	110
XII.	The New Catholicism	120
	A Prayer for Unity	131
	Notes and References	133
	Bibliography	138

Chapter I

FREEDOM IN CHRIST

THE Free Church idea is implicit in the life, teaching and work of Jesus Christ.

The Son of God—Messiah and Saviour of the world—came to Judea without benefit of Jewish hierarchal approval or announcement. The Sanhedrin, Judaism's official ruling body which controlled its religious and political life, was so completely out of touch with God's purpose and plan for the salvation of lost and sinful man that they did not even recognize the long-awaited Messiah of prophecy when He came. Indeed, they were to work "hand in glove" with Rome to destroy Him upon a cross.

Jesus held His credentials, not from the traditional bodies which Judaism acknowledged as possessing all valid religious authority, but from God Himself.

Hall Caine, in his *Life of Christ*, said,[1] "When Jesus turned to the Church of his race he found no consolation. There were two classes —the Pharisees and the Sadducees. The Pharisees had degenerated into formalists. The soul of their faith had gone out of them. The form of their religion had taken the place of the spirit. Great sticklers for the sanctity of the Sabbath. Great sticklers for the shadow of moral purity. Often great and manifest hypocrites. . . He must have looked on this empty and blazing hypocrisy. The sickening sham of it. How he afterwards scarified it! He must have seen the ways of the Sadducees.

1

They were the rationalists of the Jewish faith, believers in the law of Moses, but rejecting the Resurrection, and therefore the hope of a Messiah." The ecclesiastical Establishment and its sycophants—the priests and the Levites, the scribes and the professional scholars—were all arrayed against Him.

Jesus was a free man! He was thoroughly conscious of His divine commission and that He possessed all authority and power to accomplish it. All the resources of heaven were His and He was determined to do His Father's will regardless of the cost in human and religious relationships with the "powers that be."

Jesus was conscious of the power of Rome. He saw its governors and procurators—unprincipled and cruel men, hating, robbing, oppressing and insulting the Jews and their religion. He saw their centurions, legionnaires, auxiliaries, their prostitutes, their eunuchs, their slaves, their soldiers parading the streets ruling with whips the people once proudly known as "The Chosen." Jesus was not a Roman citizen, yet He was a free man. He was not for a moment awed by the military and political might of the greatest nation on earth.

Freedom was a mark of the man. Freedom was of the very essence of the message He proclaimed.

Jesus' first public discourse was on the subject of Freedom. He came to Nazareth (Luke 4:16-32) and stood up to read (Isaiah 61:1,2), "The Spirit of the Lord is upon me, because he hath anointed me to preach the gospel to the poor; he hath sent me to heal the brokenhearted, to preach deliverance to the captives, and recovering of sight to the blind, to set at liberty them that are bruised, to preach the acceptable year of the Lord." These were familiar words to His hearers. They were reminiscent of Leviticus 25 with the law of the Jubilee—the fiftieth year in which slaves were emancipated, lands were restored, wealth was redistributed, and the nation experienced a new birth of freedom. The Jubilee year began on the Day of Atonement and there must have been strong spiritual connotations in the minds of Jesus' hearers as He read the stirring passage. But then He staggered them by saying, "This day is the scripture fulfilled in your ears!"

This was too much for the elders of the synagogue. Was not this

Joseph's son? Why such an outlandish claim? After a brief exchange of words, tempers rose and everybody in the synagogue rose up, "thrust him out of the city," and led Him to the brow of a hill "that they might cast him down headlong," but "he passing through the midst of them went his way."

But Freedom had been proclaimed. Liberty was made the hallmark of Christ's ministry and His message.[2]

What was the nature of the freedom Christ taught? In His teaching ministry He held that liberty consists not merely in external freedom but in deliverance from sin, the darkening of the mind, the tyranny of ungodly lusts, the enthrallment of the will induced by corrupting pride and the lust for power and adulation.

Liberty, as He taught it, begins in the New Birth. It cannot exist apart from holiness and godliness, and the God-given will to do what is right and good regardless of external influences, powers and organizations.

In Psalm 119 a godly man could boast of a measure of liberty, but the Gospel of Christ truly bestows it in its fulness: Giving a full and clear knowledge of God; discovering the way of forgiveness; supplying the highest motives of holiness and the Holy Spirit; destroying the power of sin; and quickening man to righteousness. Liberty is the gift of God and cannot come from men and the creations of men. The Gospel lifts men out of the sphere of external law and gives glorious liberty or freedom in Christ.

It may be well to dwell further on this wonderful gift which Christians enjoy.

The Christian is not bound by the Law as a means of salvation. His conscience is not burdened with "Thou shalt nots." Christian liberty is the guarantee of his peace of mind. The requirements of the Law have been fulfilled in his behalf by Christ the Saviour. As Paul put it in Galatians 5:1, "For freedom did Christ free us: stand fast therefore, and be not entangled with the yoke of bondage."

Christian liberty is for the purpose of glorifying God. "Whether ye eat, or drink, or whatsoever ye do, do all to the glory of God" (I Corinthians 10:31). "And whatsoever ye do in word or deed, do all in the name of the Lord Jesus, giving thanks to God and the Father by him" (Colossians 3:17).

Christian liberty has limits. "All things are lawful," says Paul in I Corinthians 10:23, but he hastens to add that "all things are not expedient." Christian liberty ends when it operates outside the will of Christ. Without question Christian liberty is a moral gain, but whatever disrupts communion with Christ, or weakens one's desire for the guidance of the Holy Scriptures, or dulls his concern for others must be set aside.

Christian liberty ends when it is used as a stumbling block by weaker believers. The Christian will not use his "liberty for an occasion of the flesh, but (he is) by love (to) serve . . . another" (Galatians 5:13). He will exercise his freedom by the higher law of love. Love does not insist upon its own rights when it means trampling another's conscience.

Christian liberty is not to be misused in ways which might cause the Gospel or the Church to be reproached by unbelievers. "Sanctify Christ as Lord in your hearts . . . having a good conscience; that whereas they speak evil of you, as of evil doers, they may be ashamed that falsely accuse your good conversation in Christ," says the Apostle Peter in his first epistle (v. 15ff).

Christian liberty is no excuse for making common cause with un-believers (II Corinthians 6:14). There can be no intimate relation-ship between lives based on divergent premises. "Two cannot walk together except they be agreed" (Amos 3:3).

Obedience to Christ guarantees to every Christian the fullest enjoy-ment of the largest liberty. A. M. Fairbairn, in his *Revelation of Law in Scripture*, says,[3] "True liberty in the spiritual as well as the civil sphere is a *regulated* freedom; it moves within the bounds of law, in a spirit of rational obedience; and the moment these are set aside, self-will rises to the ascendant, bringing with it the witchery and dominion of sin." The Apostle Paul, whose life and writings evidence the fullest possible enjoyment of true Christian liberty, constantly uses the words "servant," "service" and "serve," to characterize his relationship to Christ. Bondage to Christ is the glad response of the Christian free-man, but it is a filial rather than a legal obedience. As we said in the beginning of our treatise, the only true freedom is the freedom which is an endowment of the New Birth. It is only after regeneration that men are free to do the will of Christ and in the doing of it find sweet release.

But in our day there are many specious brands of liberty and liberalism. Ecclesiastical leaders, comparable to those of Christ's day, have set themselves up as arbiters of truth and rulers over God's heritage. Repudiating the Christ of the Holy Scriptures, they attribute their liberal doctrines, heretical practices and revolutionary programs to "the will of Christ" and "the leadership of the Holy Spirit." They claim freedom from "the dead letter" of Scripture and access to special channels of communication with Christ vouchsafed them by their status as church officials.

Christians who are free in the Christ of the Scriptures have a right to inquire of these ecclesiastical leaders whose Christ they speak for.

Is he the Christ of Strauss, the radical theologian of the Hegelian schools, who forsook all historic tradition about him and eventually abandoned the Christian faith for a pantheistic interpretation of evolution?

Is he the Christ of Renan, the celebrated French theologian and orientalist, who rejected everything supernatural about him and became an ardent advocate of the esthetic values of religion?

Is he the Christ of tradition as expressed in the life of the historic church? If so, is he the Unitarian or the Trinitarian Christ, the Roman Catholic or the Protestant Christ?

Is he the Christ of the "divine-human encounter" of neo-orthodoxy? If so, what is his identification with the Christ of the New Testament?

Is he the Christ of "inner consciousness," a mere psychological experience, a direct and intimate encounter with a Something-or-other, not far removed from obscurantism and occultism?

If he is not the Christ of the New Testament, what matters it if his Lordship and his will are honored? He is not the Christ of God.

The fact is that these modern liberals would entangle the Church of Christ in a "yoke of bondage" comparable to that against which the Apostle Paul warned the Galatians (Galatians 5:1).

Jesus, the Christ of history, initiated the great movement which was to bear His name and change the course of world thought and action, in blithe disregard of the traditional and established cultural and religious structures of His day. The approach and method He employed to accomplish His purpose were in marked contrast to those commonly used in the affairs of men. He favored the individual approach and appealed for personal commitment, though He did not scorn the use of mass techniques for the dissemination of His ideas. Instead of asking for conferences with the Sanhedrin or the Temple scholars, He dealt individually with men like Nicodemus. Instead of seeking an official confrontation with the Samaritan hierarchy, He talked with the woman of Sychar at Jacob's well. He created no sectarian ecclesiastical organization. Though He had twelve disciples and appointed 70 men for a special mission, He set up no hierarchy to control or direct the burgeoning fellowship of His followers.

What happened during Jesus' earthly ministry was the re-establishment of the free and unencumbered fellowship between God and man, which had been broken first by the sin of Adam and later in the history of mankind by repeated social and national revolts against the will and way of God. Jesus, the Son of God, established direct *koinonia* between God and man (John 3:16). As a culmination of His ministry He was to become "the Lamb of God, who takes away the sin of the world," paying the penalty of man's rebellion against God and making it possible for man to re-establish an eternal life relationship with his Creator. In the death of Christ a way was to be provided by which we have "boldness to enter into the holiest by (his) blood, by a new and living way which he opened for us, through the veil, that is, through his flesh" (Hebrews 10:19, 20).

Christ, in His early ministry, often alluded to this fellowship in terms such as "the kingdom of God" and "the kingdom of heaven." Finally, however, He announced that He would build a Church (Matthew 16:18). He called it "my" Church. It was to preserve and perpetuate the fellowship between God and man, in vital, personal terms. In fact, the occasion which called forth His announcement was the confession of Peter to the fact that "Thou art the Christ, the son of the living God" (Matthew 16:16). Christ Himself was to be the true center of His new entity. It was to be a Christ-ianity, not a Church-ianity. The mark of identity which was to declare men to be members of His Church was personal commitment to and fellowship in Christ, not an ecclesiastical organization.

We pause to note that at no time from this event on the coast of Caesarea Philippi until the Church was actually established in Jerusalem on the Day of Pentecost, did Jesus Christ resort to any of the means usually employed in the formation of ecclesiastical organizations. He called no council of theologians. He ignored the noted priests, scribes and rabbis of Jerusalem. He did not seek approval from the Sanhedrin. He courted no favors from men of noble birth or political influence. He took no surveys to discover a strategic geographical location for a central headquarters. Indeed, His procedure was so altogether unusual that we are forced to conclude it was deliberate and intended to highlight the unique nature of His Church.

Whenever Christ had occasion to refer to this new relationship He was about to establish, He emphasized its personal character. Shortly before His death He used the allegory of the True Vine (John 15:1-8ff) as an illustration of the nature of His Church. The vine was the symbol of Israel, "not in their national but in their church capacity," says Edersheim. Also, the vine was considered to be a symbol of the Messiah. The "true vine" of which He speaks has, therefore, connotations of Jesus being the *true* Messiah; His Church, the *true* Israel of God; and Himself the *true* source of its spiritual life. The vine and its branches represent the mysterious and vital union between Christ and the individual members of His body. As the vine sends the sap into every branch causing the fruit to grow and ripen; so Christ communicates spiritual life and grace to every member of His body causing him to bring forth fruits of the Spirit and to be fruitful in every good work. Members of Christ's Church are therefore partakers of His divine nature. But the allegory has admonitions and rebukes. Branches (individual Christians) that bear no fruit are to be purged or pruned. The dead wood is to be burned. The remaining branches are expected to bring forth more fruit as a result of the cleansing. The disciplining or cleansing of the Church takes place through the Word and the sorrows, temptations, disappointments and trials which beset mankind. The angels are to gather the useless branches and destroy them. In a touching epilogue Jesus assured His disciples of His abiding love and called upon them to continue in His love. "If ye keep my commandments," He said, "ye shall abide in my love; even as I have kept my Father's commandments and abide in his love. . . Ye are my friends, if ye do whatsoever I command you. . . Ye have not chosen me, but I have chosen you, and ordained you, that ye should go and bring forth fruit, and that your fruit should remain. . ." A study of the whole 15th chapter of John in depth with special application to the ensuing events of Pentecost is most rewarding in giving new meaning to the nature of the Church, its structure and growth.

Living union with Christ, loving those who love Him without any concern for ecclesiastical structures or overlords, is in the truest and purest sense the *koinonia* and the *ecclesia* which Christ came to establish. It is not primarily a theology, a ritual or ceremony, a system or an institution. It exists wherever "two or three are gathered together" in Christ's name and where there is life union with God through Him.

When, in the fulness of time, Christ actually established His full-fledged *Ecclesia*, its nature and purpose were more precisely defined. As all true scholars agree, the Church was born on the Day of Pentecost, A.D. 30, in the city of Jerusalem, under circumstances clearly delineated in Acts 2. Christ Himself was present through the instrumentality of the Holy Spirit. There was a mystical quality about the proceedings. What was created there was the Body of Christ—a fellowship of believers cemented together in the Holy Spirit. It is often alluded to as "the fellowship of Christ" (I Corinthians 1:9) and as "the fellowship of the Holy Spirit" (II Corinthians 13:13 and Philippians 2:1). The event began in the miraculous descent of the Spirit (the last of the great saving miracles in the process of revelation). It was followed by the preaching of the Gospel by the Apostle Peter, speaking as the Spirit gave him utterance. Christ was lifted up as Saviour and Lord. There was immediate response in the hearts of the hearers, in faith believing that Christ was the Son of God, their Saviour and Lord. When they cried out asking what they must do to obtain His salvation, Peter responded by saying, "Repent and be baptized every one of you in the name of Jesus Christ for the remission of sins, and ye shall receive the gift of the Holy Spirit" (Acts 2:38). They gladly received His word and were baptized and—lo!—THE CHURCH. This new community of believers became by divine fiat the bearer of the Word and the Spirit of Christ to all mankind, and "continued steadfastly in the apostles' doctrine and fellowship, and in breaking of bread and prayers" (Acts 2:42).

Emil Brunner, in his tremendously significant volume, *The Misunderstanding of the Church*, in his chapter dealing with Pentecost and the birth of the Church, describes the relationship which exists in the true *Ecclesia*:[4]

"The Ecclesia is what it is through the presence of Christ dwelling within it. He is present with it through His Word and His Spirit— 'the spirit of truth which shall lead you into all truth.' Therefore, because the Holy Spirit is the very life-breath of the Church, the Church participates in the special character of the holy, the numinous, the supernatural, in the hallowing presence of God: for the reason that the Christian society itself is a miracle. It is therefore in point of fact unintelligible from a purely sociological standpoint. For it is in fact intelligible only from the standpoint of Christ who dwells within it and determines its life. And so because it is itself 'the temple of the Holy Spirit,' it is in its very essence the sphere of the holy and needs no Temple. The fact that it is both *koinonia Christou* or *koinonia pneumatos* and 'fellowship with one another,' thus combining the vertical with the horizontal, divine with human communion—that fact constitutes its entirety characteristic, its utterly unparalleled life.

"The togetherness of Christian men is thus not secondary or contingent: it is integral to their life just as is their abiding in Christ. But this fellowship of the society does not exist independently and in its own right: it flows from communion with Christ. For this reason we may see how impossible it is to describe the Church as a means to a higher end. The fellowship of Christians is just as much an end in itself as is their fellowship in Christ. This unique meeting of the horizontal with the vertical is the consequence and the type of that communion which the Father has with the Son 'before the world was'; in the supernatural life of the Christian communion is completed the revelation of the triune God. . . For the very being of God is *Agape*, that love which the Son brings to mankind from the Father, and it is just this love which is the essence of the fellowship of those who belong to the *Ecclesia*. Hence this love is called the 'bond of perfectness' of the *Ecclesia*."

Any creed, liturgy, tradition, doctrine, dogma, organization, office, officer, or any other creature that might intervene, hinder, impede or restrict the freedom which Christians have in Christ must be considered anathema.

Jesus Christ, the Son of God, and He alone sustains all the essential characteristics of the Church which He founded. Christ is the primary part of the edifice. Christ gives lasting stability to it. Christ makes and keeps the true unity of the Body. Upon individual personal faith in Him rests every living stone in His spiritual house. The whole system of Christianity is founded upon the Christ of God.

W. L. Hayden, who wrote the only definitive work on church polity produced in the long history of Disciples of Christ, said,[5] "When Christian believers repudiate all other authoritative creeds, and submit diverse intellects and wills to the authoritative voice and the guiding hand of the Son of God, there will be a restoration of the original unity of the Church. Faithful men who continue in the things which they have learned and been assured of, knowing that they have learned them of the only Spirit-endowed apostles of Christ, will be thoroughly furnished unto all good works so long as the Church is to endure. Thus by the institution of our Lord the building has the same sure foundation through the centuries, the Rock of Ages. He has prevailed over the gates of Hades, and defies all assaults of Satan and impious men. The wavering minds of the tempted disciples may receive divine encouragement, and their souls be confirmed by the enduring word of God through faith. The spiritual kingdom diffused throughout the earth will have the uniting power of consolidated authority of 'the blessed and only Potentate, the King of kings and Lord of lords.' The sheep will enjoy all needed watchful care and wholesome pastures, while the lambs may hear the friendly voice, be followed by the faithful searchers, and folded in the affectionate embrace of duly qualified and divinely appointed under-shepherds, until He whom Peter himself calls 'the

Shepherd and Bishop of your souls,' 'the Chief Shepherd,' shall appear, when all, pastors and flock, 'shall receive a crown of glory that fadeth not away.'"

Christians can be truly free only in Christ Jesus. Utterly dependent upon Him we have at one and the same time liberty and obligation. Entirely committed to Him and His program, we are entirely free in fellowship with others of like mind and heart. This freedom and obligation are of the essence of the Gospel of Christ and of the Church of the New Testament. Whatsoever is more than this is a false churchliness that sees in an institution a substitute for the true fellowship. For some years now we have heard the insistent slogan, "Let the Church be the Church." Implicit in it is the suggestion that the fellowship of Christians is dependent upon ecclesiastical organization and upon the exaltation of an institution which must somehow have a major place in the affections and loyalties of men. There is the further implication that since there are many so-called churches, organized unity of all the churches in a United Church is the only means by which the "wholeness" of the Church can be re-established. Advocates of this ecumenical strategy misunderstand their own deep longing for the universal fellowship of all Christians and are striving to appease it by creating an even greater ecclesiastical monstrosity to stand athwart the path toward the answer of Christ's prayer in John 17. Christ prayed only that "they all may be one; as thou, Father, art in me, and I in thee, that they also may be one in us. . . I in them, and thou in me, that they may be made perfect in one" (vs. 21, 23).

The crying need of the hour is for a new birth of freedom in Christ and a new responsibility in fellowship, far removed from all forms of structural collectivism and from a false ecclesiasticism, created though it may be, for the purpose of achieving effective communion of brethren in Christ.

For freedom did Christ free us: stand fast therefore, and be not entangled with the yoke of bondage! (Galatians 5:1).

Chapter II

THE NEW TESTAMENT CHURCH

THE Church of Christ depicted in the New Testament has an intimate relationship to Christ Himself.[1] This was realized by Luke when he wrote his history of the Church. The first part tells of Jesus' life on earth; the second describes the rise and expansion of His Church. The one dealt with His life in the flesh, the other with His life in the larger dimension of the *Ecclesia*.

Most modern church historians look upon the Church as something other than that which Christ created. They are content to examine the tree apart from its roots. They tell us about the successes, the failures, the trials and the errors, the formation of doctrines, the modes of worship and the confrontations with pagan mores and cultures which affected the development of the early Church, but they have little light to throw on the inner forces and the divine guidance which were at work to shape the Church for the accomplishment of the purposes of God. These historians persist in twisting and distorting a communion of persons with Christ into an institutional church and identifying it with human secular organizations and subjecting it to the same limitations and laws which control their growth and development. They thus admit the basic premises upon which Roman Catholicism is built. They see only the physical growth of something called "Christendom" with its burgeoning statistics, its elaborate institutions, its vast theologies, its impressive edifices, its dignified and efficient administrative systems, and its growing political power. This is not the Church that Jesus built. This ecclesiastical monstrosity is all but severed from the person and the mission of Jesus Himself and is incapable because of its very nature of expressing the true essence of Christian faith, life and work.

It is not without divine intent that the earthly manifestation of the structure of Christ's Church is marked by utter simplicity. Anything more than the structure revealed in the New Testament has a tendency to obscure and supplant the essential relationship with Christ, the Head of the Church, and the fellowship of the people of God dwelling in the Spirit. Anything more tends to deflect the life commitment of men to Church rather than to Christ.

The first community of believers to which we are introduced in the New Testament is the church at Jerusalem. Luke tells us that after Pentecost these Christians "continued steadfastly in the apostles' doctrine and fellowship, and in breaking of bread, and in prayers . . . and the Lord added to the church daily such as were being saved" (Acts 2:42, 47). It is evident that the church consisted of men whom Christ admitted into membership as soon as they were willing to accept Him as Saviour and Lord and to conform to the life that He lived and taught. The Jerusalem brethren had evidently received salvation by the justifying righteousness of His life and the atoning sacrifice of His death, and the impartation of the Holy Spirit which would enable them to live the godly life. It is likewise evident that the Jerusalem brethren recognized the fact that the Apostles had been appointed by Christ as the infallible guides in matters of doctrine and in creating the church in the form of a regular society, possessed of a definite character, with its proper rights, privileges, programs of work and practical objects. Christ had made this apostolic function clear in the encounter at Caesarea Philippi (Matthew 16:13-20), in the discourse after the Last Supper (John 14, 15, 16), in the Great Commission (Matthew 26:16-20), and at many other times in His earthly ministry.

G. A. Jacobs, in *The Ecclesiastical Polity of the New Testament*, says,[2] "The church of the apostolic period is the only church in which there is found an authority justly claiming the acknowledgment of

Christian bodies in other times. And such authority is found in this church, not because it was possessed of a truer catholicity, or a purer constitution, or a more primitive antiquity than belongs to succeeding ages, for neither antiquity, nor purity of form, nor catholicity confers the right to govern or command; but because it was under the immediate rule and guidance of the apostles, and it is their infallible judgment alone, as exhibited in the church, which has a legitimate claim to our submission. . . The authority to which alone we should appeal is that of the Divine Head of the whole Church as it may be gathered from the words and actions of His inspired apostles. The one safe and legitimate course in all church reforms is to go to the New Testament as our guide."

Paul must be considered to be a part of this divinely-appointed Apostolate. It is impossible in the limited scope of this work to deal in any depth with the problem of this unique relationship. His claim to special appointment by Christ to be the Apostle to the Gentiles was fully recognized by the Apostles of the first Jerusalem church. Scott,[3] Brunner and many other scholars in the field of church polity discuss this problem at length and agree that Paul's insights and deliverances concerning the will of Christ for His Church are of equal value to those of his companions in the faith.

As Hayden points out,[4] the Lord's prime ministers had seven characteristics which equipped them for their unique position: "(1) They saw and heard and knew the Lord Jesus Christ Himself in person; (2) They were immediately called and chosen to that office by Christ Himself; (3) Infallible inspiration was an essential requisite to the exercise of their office; (4) The power of working miracles was an indispensable qualification to the full discharge of their duties; (5) To them was specially given the power of imparting spiritual gifts and miraculous powers to others; (6) Their mission was universal—the whole world was the field of their operations; and (7) They exercised, while they lived, a superintendence over all the churches planted by their instrumentality, and their authority was paramount to that of all other functionaries." But as Brunner says,[5] "After the death of the apostles, the apostolic office retains its value in one way only: as providing the norm of the fundamental tradition now committed to writing, of the fundamental testimony, that of the New Testament. . . The Scripture is the norm of all dogma, because it crystallized the primary shape of tradition and hence becomes regulative for the teaching of the church."

Unquestionably Christ and the Apostles sanctioned the basic idea of the Jewish synagogue as a pattern in church structure. The primitive disciples were accustomed to worship in the synagogue. The synagogue is believed to have come into being during the Babylonian exile. Deprived of the Temple and having no sanctuary or altar, devout Jews gathered around their pious, God-fearing leaders knowledgeable in the Law to listen to the Word of God and engage in devotional exercises. After the exile the synagogue remained as a vital part of the Jewish religious community. Where "two or three were gathered together in the name of Jehovah God" it was permissible to have divine worship. Each group was an independent entity, the test of fellowship being commitment to the Law and the faithful practice of its precepts. Elders were chosen who had various functions. One of their number was the Ruling Elder. Then there were servants who cared for the furniture and acted as teachers. Delegates were chosen by the elders to conduct the services. This was not a permanent office, different persons were asked at various times to read the Scriptures and offer the prayers. The interpreters translated and commented upon the Scriptures. The almoners collected and distributed alms for the poor. It was not until Roman occupation of Judea that the Temple and the Sanhedrin exercised any considerable authority over the synagogues. Indeed, the very independency of the synagogues was the characteristic which made it possible for them to exist (often in homes and underground) during times of persecution and heathen domination. According to Philo,[6] synagogues were the means by which the Jews maintained their separate existence when they were far removed from their priests and scribes. He noted that these Jews were so independent in their views that they seemed opposed to the narrow interpretations of the Law which obtained in Jerusalem and free to invite whomsoever they pleased to discourse to them on the deeper issues of thought and life.

It is not strange, therefore, that church historians have marked many similarities between the synagogues and the local churches of the early Christian community. There are many instances in which Jewish Christians continued to meet in their accustomed synagogues worshipping on the seventh day in their usual manner and then after sundown, when the first day (the day of Christ's resurrection and the establishment of the Church) had come, they observed the Lord's Supper, sang their Christian hymns, joined in common worship and listened to a Gospel sermon. We are not here concerned with the manner of worship or the doctrine taught, but rather with the inescapable fact that the structure of the earliest Christian churches was congregational and without any external ecclesiastical control. They were free churches.

Leonard Bacon says,[7] "Every reader of the New Testament books may gather up for himself the hints which they give, incidentally, about the churches of Galatia, or the saints at Philippi 'with elders and deacons' or the 'churches of the Thessalonians', or 'the seven churches of Asia' or the seemingly unorganized fraternity of believers in Rome. He may observe the traces and rudiments of organization among 'the holy and faithful brethren in Christ' at Colosse, or among those whom Peter and James and the author of the Epistle to the Hebrews addressed in their writings. He may scrutinize the pastoral epistles to ascertain how far the development of ecclesiastical institutions had advanced in the latest years of the Apostle Paul. . .

"The churches instituted by the apostles were local institutions only," continues Bacon.[8] "Nothing like a national church, distinct and individual among co-ordinate national churches—nothing like a provincial church, having jurisdiction over many congregations within certain geographical boundaries, natural or political—appears in the writings or acts of the Apostles. . . But that the organized church, in the primitive age of Christianity, was always a local institution, never political or diocesan—is a proposition few will deny. . . Each local church was complete in itself and was held responsible to Christ for its own character and the character of those it retained in fellowship. . . Particular churches in that age were related to each other as constituent portions of the Universal Church. Their unity was their one faith and hope. It was the unity of common ideas and principles distinguishing them from all the world besides—of common interests and efforts, of common trials and perils, and of mutual affection. . ."

It may be rewarding to consider briefly at this point the conception of the Church revealed in the writings of Paul and primarily, of course, in his own epistles. Paul was probably the most intelligent and ecclesiastically experienced Jew among the Apostles. He was also the most cosmopolitan and widely travelled, familiar with all the theologies and philosophies of the heathen religions and cultures. He was, because of his status, even more susceptible to the temptations of ecclesiastical and hierarchical position and power than the Apostle Peter. The nature of his ministry which took him to "the ends of the earth" would seem to convince him that some strong central government might be essential to the preservation and perpetuation of the Church, scattered as it was in weak and insignificant groups under leaders who were often ill-prepared for their tasks.

The Apostle has a clear testimony about the Church. He conceived it to be based on a personal relationship of Christian individuals with Christ, resting on the principle of faith. He was conscious of immediate union of his own soul with Christ so that he could declare, "I live, yet not I, but Christ lives in me." This personal note is everywhere in Paul's teaching. Yet he was aware of the necessity of fellowship with others of like mind and heart. When he came into a new community preaching the Gospel and winning men to Christ, he led them in immediately forming a community, representing in its own locality the one indissoluble Church of Christ. For Paul the Christian religion was inseparable from the Church and almost all his letters were addressed to the churches. He was deeply concerned with the interests of the churches and he, as an Apostle, did not hesitate to give authoritative directions covering all phases of congregational life. The 12th chapter of I Corinthians is a splendid example. He thought of the Church as the Body of Christ. He declared that it was like the human body, which consists of many members, each one with its special function, while all are dependent on one another and operate in harmony. An injury to one is felt by all. The service of one organ may seem inferior to that of another, and yet if it were lacking the whole body would suffer. He saw the unity of the church as involving

diversity yet pervaded in all its parts by the one life-giving principle—Christ Himself who dwells in the Church and animates it.
If Paul gave instruction and guidance it was not as an ecclesiastical
overlord, but as a shepherd exercising in behalf of Christ a special
ministry which would soon be terminated.

Parenthetically, it is interesting to note that he was opposed to the
idea that the Church should take on the color of the current social order
and adapt itself to alien modes of thought, organization and life. He
saw the Church as the pioneer in a new concept of God-man relationships, new techniques of thought and life, new allegiances, and a new
revolution that would turn the world upside-down. To this end he
urged Christians to be a separate people. "Come ye out from among
them," he said, "and be ye separate." This did not mean that the
Church should withdraw itself from the world; it should take its place
in the world but not be *of* the world. He saw the Church as something
other than the world, standing by itself over against the world, and
drawing men out of the world into Christ and into the Church. There
is no indication that Paul had any desire to elevate or improve heathen
society. He was contending for higher goals, knowing that the inevitable result of their attainment would be to ameliorate man's individual
ills and his social problems.

In his instructions to the churches, Paul led them to constitute themselves in an orderly fashion. Claiming divine instruction, he set up a
staff of officers, described their functions, laid down rules for the conduct of worship, for works of benevolence, for congregational discipline and for spiritual growth. He thought of all the churches as a
universal spiritual brotherhood with a mutuality of concern and a
common goal. But he never indicated that the setting up of a federation of churches or a council of churches under a Bishop of Jerusalem
or Antioch, or the creation of a Super-Church exercising a species of
control over local churches was essential to this concept of the "wholeness" of the Church.

Now the question arises, Does the New Testament in the writings
of Paul and the other Apostles reveal with any clarity the pattern of
church function and polity? If the Scriptures do not furnish a pattern for what is essential in the constitution of a Christian Church, we

certainly have no trustworthy guide by which we can know that such a thing as the Christian Church now exists. The very idea of a Christian Church presupposes a knowledge of what constitutes such a church. If the Scriptures do not furnish this knowledge, then Christ and His Apostles left their posterity without any intelligent means of forming churches or of identifying churches as true Churches of Christ.

It must be admitted that the Apostles organized churches. They must have been formed by reference to certain principles and have possessed certain characteristics which warranted their being called churches. If then we can discover what Christ and the Apostles called churches, we should know what constitutes churches. Where, but in the New Testament, can this knowledge be discovered? As far as we know, God has given no other revelation of His will respecting the churches than that which the New Testament furnishes. So called "churches" which fail to bear the identifying marks of the churches described in the New Testament can scarcely qualify as true Churches of Christ. What are some of these identifying marks?

(1) There is, first of all, the whole body of believers constituting The Church Universal that is in heaven and on earth. It contains all the elect of God joined in one Lord, one Faith, one Baptism, one Hope and guided by one Rule, the Word of God. Jesus Christ is the King in this Kingdom and Head of His Church. All authority in heaven and earth has been given to Him. He is the great Shepherd and Bishop of the Redeemed. He has established the laws for the government of the Universal Church and its members constitute a Christocracy which shall forever endure.

(2) The Church, as it is seen in this present world, is "essentially, intentionally, and constitutionally one; consisting of all those in every place that profess their faith in Christ and obedience to Him in all things according to the Scriptures, and that manifest the same by their tempers and conduct, as none else can truly and properly be called Christians." Local manifestations of the visible Church are composed by the voluntary association of professed Christians united together for the worship of God and performing such other functions as become the Church of Christ, and governed by the system of local church organization and administration established by the Apostles of Christ.

Where the Apostles have bound them, they are bound to observe their directions; where they have left them free, they are at liberty to make their own arrangements.

(3) The functions of a local church, according to the New Testament, are (a) to glorify Christ (Ephesians 5:25-27); (b) to worship God in spirit and in truth (Hebrews 10:19-25); (c) to preach the Gospel (I Corinthians 15:1-11); (d) to observe the sacraments of baptism and the Lord's Supper (Romans 6, I Corinthians 11); (e) to supply instruction in righteousness (Ephesians 4:11-16); (f) to exercise discipline (II Thessalonians 3:6-15); (g) to provide fellowship and Christian growth (Romans 15:1-7, Ephesians 2:14-22); (h) to minister to the unfortunate (James 1:27, Acts 6:1-7); (i) to seek the lost (Matthew 28:16-20); and (j) to promote Christian unity (I Corinthians 1:10, Romans 14:19).

(4) The rule of discipline of the local church is the New Testament. Two principles are evident here: the New Testament is the only rule of faith and practice to the exclusion of all human creeds, canons, traditions and philosophies; and private judgment or interpretation is the right and duty of all. The Christian is thus freed from all human authority in religion and is bound only by divine authority. It rescues him from clerical interpretation and fully recognizes his personal responsibility to God. Emphasis on the New Testament does not in any way repudiate the validity of the Old Testament as the Word of God, but it makes the New the only law of the Christian Church. It abolishes Jewish rites and ceremonies that were a "shadow of things to come." It retains all the enduring principles of God's moral government which are the same in all ages. In the free church the New Testament becomes a rule of faith. As Thomas Campbell expressed it,[9] "Nothing ought to be inculcated upon Christians as articles of faith, nor required of them as terms of communion, but what is expressly taught and enjoined upon them in the Word of God. Nor ought anything to be admitted as of divine obligation in the church constitution and managements, but what is expressly enjoined by the authority of our Lord Jesus Christ and His Apostles upon the New Testament Church, either in expressed terms or by approved precedent." The New Testament becomes in the free church the rule

of *faith* and *practice*, involving the conduct of Christians; the observance of the ordinances or sacraments and acts of worship; and the discipline or government of the Church. If the Church realizes the all-sufficiency of the inspired Scriptures and becomes proficient in a correct understanding of their teaching, it will prosper in all those things which are its chief concern.

(5) Congregational rights are based on the equality of all Christians before God. All are on the same level of privilege and enjoy a common fellowship. There is neither male nor female; all are one in Christ Jesus. The universal priesthood of believers obtains. It involves the right and privilege of every disciple of Christ to participate in an orderly way in all congregational acts. Bound together by mutual covenant in Christ as a congregation, Christians possessed, under Him, self-completeness and the right of self-government. Congregational autonomy makes it possible to transact all essential business of a Christian Church, settle all questions of expediency, choose all necessary officers possessing scriptural qualifications and deposing them if they become disqualified. All matters with the exception of faith, piety and morality or apostolic directive are appropriate for congregational consideration and decision.

Numerous passages of Scripture in the New Testament mention positions of leadership which the Apostles recognized as important in the life of the churches. Among these references are I Corinthians 12:27-31, Ephesians 4:11-13, I Timothy 3:1-13, Titus 1:5-9, and I Peter 5:1-4. The *Apostles* were charged with the unique mission of establishing the Church with all its essential ministries to edify, extend and perpetuate it to the end of time. When they died the apostolic office ceased. The *prophets* had a unique ministry essential to the life of the Church in its formative period. *Miracle workers* and *tongue-speakers* likewise fulfilled a purpose until the revelation of God was completed and the Word of Faith was available to all in the New Testament. The remaining church leaders mentioned in these passages of Scripture are the permanent teachers and leaders in the Church today.

(6) The *evangelist* has an important ministry in the conversion of the lost and the establishment of new churches. He is a proclaimer

of the Gospel beyond the limits of the local churches. The New Testament books of Timothy and Titus were written by the Apostle Paul to two evangelists. Others in the same class were Barnabas, Silvanus, Tychicus, Aquila, Apollos, Aristarchus, and Epaphroditus. Alexander Campbell taught that "evangelists constitute the living itinerant ministry of the church sent abroad into the world and sustained in their labors by the church. They preach the word of life. They convert the world. They institute churches and set them in order." Missionaries who carry the Gospel to the ends of the earth fall into this category. Local churches are primarily responsible for instructing, choosing, ordaining and supporting evangelists and missionaries.

(7) *Elders* (sometimes called pastors, presbyters, bishops, overseers or teachers) are charged with the shepherding, instruction, discipline and direction of the local church. The church at Jerusalem had elders. When the church at Antioch sent relief to the brethren in Judea, the contribution was sent to the elders at Jerusalem. Sixteen years later, at the time of another famine, Paul went to Jerusalem to deliver to the elders the contributions of the churches of Galatia, Achaia and Macedonia. Elders among the Jews were rulers of the people and it is significant that the synagogue term was appropriated by the Christian churches. The word elder, as an official term, expresses the idea of government by men of age, prominence, experience and wisdom. It indicates that the office is one involving highly important duties and grave responsibilities. Pastors and bishops are elders who have been given special oversight, but as in the case of other elders, they are chosen by the local church and are warned in Scripture not to "lord it over God's heritage" (I Peter 5:3). The title "bishop" has been woefully misused in the history of Christendom. In its New Testament sense it carries no authorization beyond the local congregation and even in the churches there was a plurality of bishops or elders. The duties of elders are described in the New Testament as preaching, teaching, instruction, confutation and exhortation. They are to speak the Word of God, confute error and establish the truth of the Gospel in the hearts and consciences of men. The entire work of teaching or instruction in the church is under the control and direction of the eldership. Another class of duties includes management, watch-care, ad-

monition and discipline that all things in the local church be done "in decency and in order."

(8) A second officer of the Church is the *deacon*. The original appointment of deacons was by the church in Jerusalem and is recorded in Acts 6:1-6. They were ordained and charged with the special duty of ministering to the needy. Paul addressed the "saints at Philippi, with bishops and deacons" in his epistle to the church there (Philippians 1:1), indicating that it was the practice of all the churches to have deacons. Timothy was advised of the qualification and duties of deacons in I Timothy 3:1-15. It is the custom of the churches to charge its deacons with benevolent, financial and other matters of a business nature.

(9) Another important leader in the local church is the *teacher*. Pastors and teachers stand forth in the list of church leaders in Ephesians 4:11. All elders should be apt to teach, but the task of Christian education in the local church is so important that many teachers with special capabilities are needed to serve all those who are the responsibility of the church to instruct and train. Evidently the early churches had a multiplicity of teachers "learned in the Scriptures" and "able to exhort in sound teaching and to convict the gainsayers" by a clear and faithful presentation of the truth of God's Word, building up every Christian in the holy faith and converting others to the truth which is in Christ Jesus.

(10) While all the churches mentioned in the New Testament were of equal standing and complete within themselves to discharge all churchly functions, they recognized certain common concerns and had communion with one another in these matters if so led by the Spirit of God. They realized that they were all united in Christ and that they should exhibit this fellowship to one another in affording relief in times of trial, in consultation regarding difficult matters requiring the best judgment and council of others, in contributing to the general welfare of the churches, and in sending out evangelists and missionaries. An example of this fellowship is to be found in Acts 15 when the church at Antioch appealed to the church in Jerusalem for help in solving a controversy which had arisen between Jewish and Gentile Christians. In a council including "apostles, elders and brethren" to-

gether with Paul and Barnabas a possible solution was reached and recommended to the churches.   The incident had in it none of the circumstances of modern extra-congregational ecclesiastical councils and the decision reached had only the weight of good advice.[10]

(11) The Church of Christ depicted in the New Testament is a glorious fellowship.   It is world-wide in its offers of peace and pardon, and invites to its privileges, sacrifices and honors whoever wills to accept them in every family, tribe and nation.   It is not primarily an organization, but an *ecclesia*—the called out from the world who have chosen Christ as Lord and Saviour through faith in Him and obedience to His authority.   All its churches and communities are branches of the true Vine and have vital union in Christ, growing and bearing fruit according to "the law of the Spirit of life" in Him.   This Scriptural conception of the unity of the Christian Church is not realized in any human extra-congregational ecclesiastical organization, but alone in Christ, to whom be the glory!

Chapter III

THE RISE OF CATHOLICISM

FOR two hundred years after the death of the Apostles, the churches of Christ were free—congregational in polity. This fact is amply attested in the writings of the Patristic Fathers[1] who were contemporary with the Apostles or their immediate disciples.

Clement of Rome addresses his epistle (A.D. 64-70) in a manner that denotes the independence of the churches:[2] "The church of God which is at Rome, to the church of God which is at Corinth, elect, sanctified by the will of God through Jesus Christ our Lord: grace and peace. . ." He speaks of the Corinthian church as "gathered together,"[3] as composed of professed saints, as "the flock of Christ"[4] and "the sheepfold of Christ"[5] in the sense of completeness. He mentions the fact that it has "elders set over it"[6] as in the days of the Apostles and that they were chosen with "the consent of the whole church."[7] The episcopal form of government was clearly not in force at that time, although Clement in some of his statements employs the "language of Ashdod."

Polycarp, writing around A.D. 108-117, apologizes to the church at Philippi in the introduction to his epistle:[8] "These things, my brethren, I took not the liberty to write unto you concerning righteousness, but you yourselves encouraged me to it." He tells the church[9] that it is their duty to be "subject to the elders and deacons as unto God and Christ," but warns the elders to "be compassionate and merciful towards

25

all; turning them from their errors; . . . being zealous of what is good. . ." He speaks of Valens, once an elder, who has been disciplined by the congregation. He speaks of the churches as separate congregational bodies and not as subject to the authoritative direction or instruction by any one outside their body.

The epistles of Ignatius,[10] written about A.D. 107-116, indicate a change beginning to take place. He mentions an elder being appointed from each church to be a *princeps inter pures* among equals. He was called an overseer or bishop. Ignatius recognizes, however, the autonomy of the local churches in Ephesus, Magnesia, Tralles, Philadelphia, Rome and Smyrna. The kind of overseer of which Ignatius speaks evidently was associated with other elders and deacons in a local church, not a diocesan church, and without the slightest authority over other churches. These "ruling elders" recognized the right of the churches to elect and set apart to their service such elders and deacons as they desired. Ignatius indicates that these overseers were upon occasion to be "sent abroad," but for what purpose remains obscure.

The epistle of Barnabas,[11] written soon after the destruction of Jerusalem, is in tone and style similar to Clement. He makes no mention of any order of elders, thus intimating that the churches remained at the close of the first century in their organization and government very much as they were in the days of the Apostles.

Hermas, a reputed contemporary of Ignatius, says nothing in his Commands and Similitudes to support Ignatius' idea of "ruling elders." In fact, he mentions[12] in his eleventh Command the right of the congregation to admit to the pulpit any man who "hath the spirit of God."

Coming down to a still later period, we have the "Apology for Christians" written by Justin Martyr to Antonius Pius, the Roman Emperor and his two sons, about A.D. 150. This letter describes faithfully the simplicity of the worship and practices of a local congregation of Christians. It shows that piety was essential to church membership; that an open profession of faith was required after which baptism and the Lord's Supper were administered; that the church to which Christians were admitted was congregational in form of government; that there were two kinds of officers—a president and deacon; that the work assigned to the president was similar to that of a pastor or minister; that deacons distributed the elements of the Lord's Supper and ministered to the poor.

As late as A.D. 250 Cyprian wrote epistles which reflect considerable change in church practice. In one passage, however, he says,[13] "The people, obedient to the commands of our Lord, and fearing God, ought to separate themselves from a wicked bishop, nor take part with worship of a sacrilegious priest, since they especially have the power of choosing the worthy priests and of rejecting the unworthy. Which power comes from Divine authority, that a priest should be chosen in the presence of the people, and before the eyes of all, and approved by public judgment and testimony, as a fit and worthy person . . ." In Epistle V, Cyprian declines to rule on a question submitted to him[14] because "from the very commencement of my ministry I have resolved to do nothing privately, of my own mind, without your advice, and the consent of the people." This testimony to the congregational autonomy of the primitive churches comes with striking importance because Cyprian is widely quoted as a defender of the episcopacy which had arisen in the churches during the course of the third century.

Mosheim in his *Ecclesiastical History* reflects his Lutheran bias in many matters, but this is all the more reason to value his admissions as to the nature of the primitive church. Under the general heading, "History of the Teachers and of the Government of the Church," he says: "In the primitive times each Christian church was composed of the people, the presiding officers and the assistants or deacons. The highest authority was in the people, or the whole body of Christians; for even the apostles themselves inculcated by their example, that nothing of any moment was to be done or determined on, but with the knowledge and consent of the brotherhood (Acts 1:15; 6:3; 15:4; 21:22). And this mode of proceeding, both prudence and necessity required, in those early times. The assembled people, therefore, elected their own rulers and teachers; or, by their authoritative counsel, received them when nominated to them. They also by their suffrages rejected or confirmed the laws that were proposed by their rulers, in their assemblies . . . in a word, the people did everything that is proper for those in whom the supreme power of the community is vested.

"In this manner," continues Mosheim, "Christians managed ecclesiastical affairs, so long as their congregations were small, or not very numerous. Three or four presbyters, men of gravity and holiness, placed over these little societies, could easily proceed with harmony, and needed no head, or president. But when the churches became larger, and the number of presbyters and deacons, as well as the amount of duties to be performed increased, it became necessary that a council of presbyters should have a president; a man of distinguished gravity and prudence, who should distribute among his colleagues their several tasks, and be, as it were, the central point of the whole society . . . But whoever supposes that the bishops of the first and golden age of the church, corresponded with the bishops of the following centuries, must blend and confound characters that are very different. For in this century and the next, a bishop had charge of a single church which might, ordinarily, be contained in a private house; nor was he its head, but was in reality its minister and servant . . ."

Beginning in the third century a tragic change takes place — an orientation away from *Christ* and definitely toward *Church*. What the Apostles called the *Ecclesia* was the sphere of actual and realized fellowship with Christ. It was a fellowship of those united with each other through Christ and was as real as their zealous and brotherly love of each other, as were the sacrifices which they made to each other in money and property, time, strength, security and life. This fellowship was not mediated through any ecclesiastical hierarchy or organization. It refused to allow any authoritarian office, but took as its norm for church life the spirit of mutual service.[15] It recognized as valid only such human and temporal organization as was essential to the order and well being of that fellowship. It is passing strange, therefore, that out of this simple spiritually oriented complex an episcopal or catholic church would develop with an inordinate accent on ecclesiastical structure. What caused this change?

First of all, there was a very evident loss of spiritual power. The Apostle John had sensed this trend and prophetically expressed his concern in his messages to the seven churches (Revelation 2 and 3). The message to Laodicea is especially significant in this respect. Then, there was a vast increase in the number of Christians. It is probable that as Christianity became a more popular religion and persecution decreased, many people were admitted to membership who were not sufficiently indoctrinated as to their essential spiritual relationship to Christ or the deeper meaning of the ordinances.

Into this situation came the gnostic heresies and other apostasies. In self-defense came the first creeds, definitions of dogma and official norms for church teaching. The eventual tendency was for faith to be placed in doctrinal statements to such a degree as to obscure individual commitment to and communion with Christ. Men well versed in theology and church tradition came to occupy positions of prominence far beyond their local churches.

It was natural, then, that an extra-congregational episcopal office came into being. It, too, was looked upon as a protective barrier. Bishops could speak with greater authority. They could interpret Scripture more intelligently than the unlearned *hoi polloi*. They could issue pronouncements, make fixed regulations, lay down unambiguous relationships of superiority and subordination. With such leadership the fundamental and primitive testing of Christian doctrine by Scripture was neglected bringing attendant ignorance of the true teaching of the Word of God and an apathy concerning individual responsibility. Episcopacy actually transformed, in the wrong direction, the innermost spirit of the thing it desired to protect.

Church historians with a penchant for explaining ecclesiastical change in terms of social, economic, cultural and psychological development advance other reasons for the restructuring of the Church; such as, (1) a movement from economic poverty to economic wealth; (2) from cultural deprivation to cultural fulfillment; (3) from emphasis on piety to emphasis on social compatibility; (4) from charismatic fervor in worship to ritualistic forms; (5) from "leadings of the Spirit" to fixed ecclesiastical orders; (6) from emphasis on religion in the home to institutionally oriented religion; (7) from a persecution to a success psychology; (8) from a separatist conservatism to an emerging and expanding liberalism; (9) from a crusading militancy to peaceful coexistence; and (10) from a democratic spirit to an acceptance of authoritarian organization.[16]

Whatever the motivating causes for this revolutionary change in the structure of the Church adduced by scholarly observers, we must not overlook the possibility of selfish ambition and lust for power on the part of church leaders. "Ambition," said Machiavelli, "is so powerful a passion in the human breast that however high we reach we are never satisfied." Power "like a devastating pestilence, pollutes whate'er it touches." Says Shelley, it is "the bane of all genius, virtue, freedom and truth making slaves of all men, and of the human frame, a mechanized automation." A survey of the history of the Catholic church through the centuries reveals innumerable examples of ecclesiastical ambition, pride and imperialism which are a blight on the good name of Christianity.

The term "Catholic Church" first occurs about A.D. 110 or 115 in the epistle of Ignatius to the Smyrneans (8:2): "Wherever the bishop shall appear, there let also the multitude be, even as wherever Christ may be, there is the Catholic Church." The passage gives no evidence of the existence of the ecclesiastical institution which later developed, but it does indicate a trend of thought which eventuated in a specious justification of such an institution. Ignatius was saying that the presence of the official overlord and the acknowledgment of his authority is the visible test which shows that congregations are a part of the world-wide Church of which Christ is the universal head. Bishops like Ignatius were beginning to say that the unity, universality and wholeness of the Church depend upon something other than the Spirit, something other than the local church, something that is extra-congregational and can only be made visible through an ecclesiastical hierarchy. The term "Catholic Church" then came to mean a Super-Church not limited to any locality, province or country but diffused and controlled by a universal centralized authority.

By the time of the third century centers of ecclesiastical power had developed[17] in the patriarchal sees of Rome, Constantinople, Antioch, Alexandria and Jerusalem. Churches in these areas came to recognize the bishops, patriarchs or metropolitans who presided over these sees as the sources of authority (rather than the Holy Scriptures) in all matters of doctrine and life. Area bishops assumed control of the ministry or clergy claiming the sole right of ordination and direction. Only interpretations of Scripture and tradition approved by the bishops were permitted to be taught in the churches.

The pre-eminence of the Bishop of Rome was inevitable in the Roman Empire which covered the entire known world. Means of communication depended upon Rome. Its political control was everywhere acknowledged. The Christian community in the city of Rome and its contiguous provinces was the largest in the world. Its internationalism was shown by its continuing for about two centuries to use the Greek language instead of the Latin. Constantly reinforced by immigration as well as by conversions, the Roman churches, including many persons of wealth, were able to support an elaborate ecclesiastical system with seven orders of clergy. The Bishop of Rome was noted for his benevolence and generosity, sending money, food and clothing to the poor churches in the sees of his rivals and making Christian service the root of his growing ecclesiastical power. This situation led to shameful rivalry among the bishops. Eventually two rose to major eminence — Rome and Constantinople.

Rome's claim to supremacy was immensely enhanced by the accession of Constantine (A.D. 306-337) to the throne of the Roman Empire. The imposing arch of Constantine built to commemorate the Emperor's victory over Maxentius, stands today as a mute witness to the fourth century as the turning point, not only of his rise to power, but of the fortunes of the Roman Church. Two centuries after this almost unbelievable transition Roman primacy was so entrenched that Catholic Christianity became the law of the Empire.

Constantine saw the Church as the means of advancing his popularity and political power and uniting the Empire in a universally accepted ideology. In A.D. 313 he issued the Edict of Milan providing that "everyone may have license to worship whatever he pleases." This act of toleration brought relief from persecution to the Christian community, but it implied imperial protection and raised the old question, "Christ or Caesar — which?" The problem of the spiritual versus the secular touched off a new wave of debate over all the theological problems which now threatened to divide the churches. The Emperor intervened, and called the Council of Nicea (A.D. 325) and gave orders that all Christian bishops attend, forthwith settle their differences, and present a united front on all matters of Christian faith and life. Thus was added to the developing Church the technique of "conciliar unity" and the tradition of the Councils as powerful factors in the ecumenical life of the churches. Another contribution that this pagan Emperor (he was baptized by Eusebius in A.D. 337, only days before his death) made to the Roman Church was his decision to move the capital of the Empire to Byzantium (Constantinople) on the Bosporus. This left the Bishop of Rome with his immense powers in virtual control of the "City of God," the "New Jerusalem" on the Tiber. He transferred his residence to the home of the Emperor's wife on the Caelian hill, built a magnificent basilica and reigned like a monarch in his own right.

The price that the Roman Church paid for this ascent to the ecclesiastical and political power can scarcely be imagined. Worshippers of the sun were placated by having the traditional Christian holy day named Sun-day. By law (321 A.D.) the observance of the "venerable day of the Sun" was required and church leaders hailed Constantine's act as initiating "a new era in the history of the Lord's Day." Heresy, previously punishable only by excommunication, was made a crime against the State and punishable by death, thus paving the way for the bloody Inquisition and the later martyrdom of millions who sought to serve only Christ. Constantine, in order to make Christianity attractive to the heathen, transferred into the Church their religious ornaments and symbols. Pagan temples were dedicated to the Apostles and the Patristic Fathers. Votive offerings were introduced as were incense, candles, lamps and holy water. Asylums, holy days and seasons with indulgences for sin became common. Processions, sacerdotal vestments, the tonsure, and jewelled rings and badges of ecclesiastical office rivalled those of the priests in pagan temples. At a later date came images of Christ and the saints, the ecclesiastical chants and the Kyrie Eleison, all of pagan origin, and sanctified by their adoption into the Church. Thus was the gate opened for penance to take the place of repentance, sprinkling and pouring to become baptism, and the eucharist to become a constantly recurring atoning altar sacrifice with mediatorial value for the living and the dead. The sign of the cross, prayers for the dead and the veneration of martyrs developed into the crucifix, purgatory and saint worship.

With the Fall of Rome in 476 A.D. and the breakdown of the Roman Empire, the Church succeeded to what might be described as "the grave of the deceased Empire" appropriating much of the paraphernalia of power which had been exercised by the Emperors, even to the orders and levels of authority. Since the outside world, apart from its super-natural certainty, was in chaos, death and beyond hope, the Roman bishop moved into the vacuum and in effect became the ruler of the temporal world. It was only a short step from this stance to that of the Papacy. Gregory I assumed the headship of Christendom (A.D. 590-604), became the "vicar of Christ on earth," and completed the program of Restructure which made the only true Church the Roman Catholic Church and the Pope its infallible Head. Indeed, as the *Larger Catechism* puts it, "All those who do not acknowledge the Roman Pontiff as their head, do not belong to the Church of Jesus Christ."

The two great apologists for "the one true Church" (the Roman Catholic Church) are Augustine (A.D. 354-430) and Gregory the Great. There is much of value in Augustine's theology with its emphasis on grace and its apparent opposition to salvation by human merit, but he identified the channels of grace with the sacraments and ministrations of the Roman Catholic Church which he considered to be the one holy, universal and apostolic Church. Gregory saw the Church as a sacred institution resting on a priestly office that exercised the powers of an episcopal ruler. Levels of power inevitably called for supreme power to be held by a Priest of Priests, a Bishop of Bishops, uniting the whole sacred character of the Church in a Person who would be the Vicar of Christ on earth. They are largely responsible for setting up the four traditional tests by which it can be determined what makes the "True Church:"

(1) It is a *United Church* because all of its members, in response to the desire of Christ, profess the same faith, have the same sacrifices and sacraments and are united under one visible head, the Pope.

(2) It is a *Holy Church* "because it was founded by Jesus Christ, and because it teaches, according to the will of Christ, holy doctrines, and provides the means of leading a holy life."

(3) It is a *Universal Church* because "destined to last for all time," it fulfills the command of Christ to go forth and make disciples of all nations, and it teaches everywhere today the same doctrine which it first received from Christ.

(4) It is an *Apostolic Church* because it is the church that Christ founded upon the Apostles, particularly Peter, whom He called the Rock on which He would build His Church. This power Peter has passed down through the centuries in unbroken line of his successors in the see of Rome. Says the *Catechism of Christian Doctrine*,[18] "We know that no other church but the Catholic Church is the true Church of Christ because no other church has these four marks."

Yet the history of this monstrous ecclesiasticism clearly reveals that:

(1) *Unity* has not been achieved by its ecclesiastical structure. In 1054 the Eastern churches split from the Western. The Greek Orthodox Catholics have every claim to uninterrupted growth from the primitive Church of Apostolic times that Rome can deduce. Other schisms came from rival parties in the church electing their partisan popes, the greatest division lasting from 1378-1429 with rival popes enthroned at Rome and Avignon. In the fifteenth century it spawned the Reformation when thousands of churches repudiated the authority of the Pope and turned to Christ alone as the Head of the Church and the Holy Scriptures as their all-sufficient guide.

(2) *Holiness* has not been achieved by ecclesiastical means. The Roman Church has been notorious for its moral degeneracy involving even its popes and many of the princes of the Church.

(3) The Roman Church cannot claim *universality* because it bears the provincial name, "Rome," is tied to Roman tradition, accepts a Roman theology and is ruled by Italian popes.

(4) Its boast of *Apostolicity* is farcical. The best proof of this is a careful reading of those passages of the New Testament which describe the Church as it existed in the days of the Apostles and a comparison of it with the Roman Catholic Church today in every aspect of its

doctrine, organization and life. The Roman Church is simply not the Church of the New Testament by the widest stretch of the imagination.

Indeed, by developing the ecclesiastical element to its utmost pitch of perfection, the Roman Church has succeeded in changing the very essence of Christian fellowship as it existed in the Apostolic Church; in distorting and contradicting every thesis of basic New Testament truth; in robbing its communicants of all those freedoms implicit in Christ; and in preventing, by erecting innumerable ecclesiastical and dogmatic stumbling blocks, the achievement of the only unity for which Christ prayed.

The rise of Catholicism, particularly that brand which bears the stamp of Rome, is a powerful living demonstration of the fact that true Christianity is not to be found in a well-developed system of rules, regulations, rituals or ecclesiastical structures. Christ tried to teach His disciples that the true religion was not limited by the four walls of a Temple in Jerusalem and did not depend on outward forms such as rabbinical laws, rituals, ceremonial sacrifices, sanhedrins or various orders of a priesthood. They learned the lesson, but with the rise of Catholicism came a sad reversion to the deadly errors of the past and the near-destruction of the Church that Jesus built.

Chapter IV

THE FREE CHURCH TRADITION

T HE Free Church has had an unbroken existence in Christendom from the first Christian Church in Jerusalem, A.D. 30, to the present day. It will be the purpose of this chapter to trace its course through the dark days of the restructured Church to the rise of the Restoration Movement in America in the early days of the nineteenth century.

Church historians have been strangely silent on this phase of the history of the Christian Church, largely due to two facts: (1) the imperialistic Roman Catholic Church slew in cold blood those who dared to oppose its ecclesiastical system and destroyed as many of their writings as they could obtain, and (2) most church historians were members of churches whose polity is basically dependent upon principles inherent in the Roman Catholic episcopacy. But now modern archeologists, researchers and free-lance pioneering scholars have uncovered vast areas of new data regarding the free churches. I shall draw upon these reliable resources in this necessarily brief and limited survey.

E. H. Broadbent, in *The Pilgrim Church,* says,[1] "Departure from the original pattern given in the New Testament for the churches met very early with strenuous resistance, leading in some cases to the formation within the decadent churches of circles which kept themselves free from the evil and hoped to be a means of restoration to the whole. Some of them were cast out and met as separate congregations. Some, finding conformity to the prevailing conditions impossible, left and formed fresh companies. These would often reinforce those others which, from the beginning, had maintained primitive practice. There is frequent reference in later centuries to those churches that had adhered to Apostolic doctrine, and which claimed unbroken succession of testimony from the time of the Apostles. They often received, both before and after the time of Constantine, the name of Cathars, or Puritans, though it does not appear that they took this name themselves."

Though the New Testament Canon as we know it today was not in these early centuries available to the churches, many of the books included in the Canon were in circulation and had been by consensus of holy men accepted by the churches as valid Apostolic guidance in all matters of doctrine, organization and life. Although copies of these books were available only in limited numbers, and Roman and Greek Catholic Church authorities did not permit individual interpretation of the Scriptures, sufficient copies were available for the guidance of the faithful churches and to enable intelligent men to know the truth and detect ecclesiastical error.

In the fourth century (A.D. 350-385) Priscillian,[2] a Spaniard of wealth and position, an eloquent and learned man, was converted to Christianity. He immediately began a study of the apostolic writings and became so proficient in them that he was made Bishop of Avila. Insisting upon strict adherence to the New Testament pattern, Priscillian soon encountered the opposition of the clerics led by Bishop Hydatius, Metropolitan of Lusitania. Finally he and his followers, called the "Priscillianists," were convicted of heresy, and despite the protests of Martin of Tours and Ambrose of Milan, Priscillian and six others were beheaded, including a distinguished lady, Euchrotia, widow of a well-known poet and author.

Vigilantius of Lyons[3] in Aquataine and presbyter of the church in Barcelona challenged Jerome (A.D. 396-406) concerning departures of Roman Catholicism from the apostolic faith. This happening is of major significance since the Waldensian protestant movement claims it to be the beginning of their existence, still maintained in the Tyrolean Alps and Italy. Vigilantius wrote from a region "between the Adriatic and the Alps of King Cotius," a region which, as Faber points out, "formed a part of what was once styled Cisalpine Gaul" and has always been noted as an area of free church influence.

Whatever may be said to discount the ministry of Montanus,[4] who, if he were living today would undoubtedly be identified with the Pentecostal movement, it must be recognized that he was an outstanding advocate of the free church idea. Montanism grew most rapidly in western North Africa and Egypt although it won adherents in Gaul and Asia Minor. No less a personality than Tertullian was won over to the new faith and wrote masterfully in its defense. The movement flourished remarkably from the latter part of the second century to 407 A.D. when Emperor Honorius decreed the death penalty for all Montanists.

The free-church ideas of the Marcionites[5] brought them into immediate conflict with the Bishops. Marcion, prosperous owner of ships from Asia Minor, separated from the institutional church about 140 A.D. Marcion held that the Church should follow the New Testament pattern in polity and rejected the Old Testament because (among other things) it furnished the ground for the sacerdotal system which was rapidly developing in the churches. The movement was marked by a strict moralism and piety and made a strong impression on the main Church, especially when Marcionites were subjected to martyrdom by the ruling Bishops. Celsus and Justin around the beginning of the third century marvelled that the movement had "spread over the whole world." Its centers of strength were in western Asia Minor, Corinth, Crete, the large cities of Antioch, Alexandria and Edessa, and even as far as Lyons and Carthage. As late as the fourth and fifth centuries Rome was warning the churches against this heresy and murdering hundreds of its followers in cold blood.

In the early centuries of the Christian Era, Milan, situated in the midst of the plain at the foot of the Alps, assumed a free church stance.[6] For hundreds of years the Bishop of Milan refused to pledge subservience to Rome. The nearby Alpine valleys and foothills were inhabited by many "seekers for liberty" and advocates of local church autonomy. The older usages and beliefs of the Church persisted. According to the claims of the later Waldenses, these congregational-type churches resisted Rome's persecutions forming a citadel "fashioned by Providence" against all attempts to erode Apostolic Christianity. As late as A.D. 555 Pope Pelagius complained that the Bishop of Milan would not come to Rome for ordination and admitted that "this was an ancient custom of theirs." In A.D. 590 several bishops of northern Italy refused to adhere to the decisions of the Council of Chalcedon.[7] Their independency formed a serious challenge to those who would restructure the Church in such a manner as to give ecclesiastical supremacy to Rome. Eventually in the eleventh century the Bishop of Milan succumbed to the immense ecclesiastical pressures and the threats of armed force brought by Rome, but the people of the Alpine mountains and the valleys refused to follow his example.

Out of this background, and undoubtedly related to it in historical sequences, came the Waldenses.[8] Their free spirit, their ancient and honorable ancestry, their devotion to Apostolic Christianity have earned them immortality in Whittier's charming miniator and Milton's moving sonnet. Their name comes from that of Peter Waldo,[9] wealthy lace merchant of Lyons, who gave his fortune to the poor, joined the "Poor Men of Lyons," and moved out across Europe to restore the New Testament Church in doctrine, ordinances and life.

The question of Waldensian origins[10] has suffered from a scarcity of source materials, but for centuries the Waldenses have contended that their free-church tradition is from Jerusalem. The Bull of Pope Lucius III (1181) admits their connection with earlier "heresies"; so does Stephen of Bourbon (1225), Burchard of Ursperg (1229), Rescriptum (1230), Salvus Bruce (1235), Moneta of Cremona (1244), David of Augsburg (1274), the Inquisition of Carcasonne (14th century), Peter the Inquisitor (1398), and many other knowledgeable sources of these early times. The older Protestant historians, such as D'Aubignes, were led in their zeal to find in the Waldenses a "visible apostolic succession" but sometimes they exceeded their limited historical source materials. Early Catholic historians, such as Bossuet,[11] are a unit in confining Waldensian history to Waldo and his successors. But further research into the field of "medieval heresies" has made it growingly clear that the Waldenses have unquestionable relationships to the earliest evangelical movements of Christendom. The English historian Beard[12] says, "The more accurate research of recent years traces the origins of the Waldenses to a double fountain, the streams of which soon mingled, and were thenceforth hard to distinguish. On the one hand, there are the Vaudois, the 'men of the valleys,' who still hold their ancient seats in the mountains of Dauphine and Piedmont; on the other, the so-called 'poor men of Lyons,' the followers of Peter Waldo . . . But the Waldenses, whatever their origin, were from the first Biblical Christians. They translated the Scriptures into their own tongue, and expounded them in their natural sense only. They maintained the universal priesthood of the believer."

Preaching by laymen (even by women) had its inception in the Waldensian movement. The preaching fellowship developed into a free church fellowship. Free societies were organized and whether in a single community or in a wider area were called "congregations." In times of persecution these cells of faith went underground and because of their fluid nature were able to maintain themselves as a continuing Church. Worship services were maintained in conventicles, and study groups assembled in little *scholae* for the edification of the brethren and the indoctrination of converts. It is true that Waldo at one time assumed the title of Bishop and claimed authority over the "congregations," but he was repudiated in this claim. Gunnar Westin says, "Of all the groups the Medieval Roman Church attempted to condemn, this free church organization was the strongest and most effective." The attempts to stop the Waldensian preachers and evangelists by prohibition and banishment failed and the Roman Church was finally driven to overt persecution. From 1211 to 1214 thousands of Waldenses were burned at the stake in France and Germany. In several countries the movement was nearly wiped out. Even in northern Italy they were driven into the fastnesses of the Alps and an underground existence. Today the Waldensian Church in Italy exhibits many of the characteristics of the old churches of the twelfth century. It is an altogether unique free church movement and in its prepetuity illustrates the strength and spiritual power inherent in it.

It is widely believed that refugee Waldenses from continental Europe were responsible for the rise of the Lollards[13] in England in the thirteenth and fourteenth centuries. John Wycliffe's work,[14] beginning about 1370, may have been inspired by this movement. He was strongly influenced at Oxford by Thomas of Bradwardine, an Augustinian theologian who was extremely critical of Rome. Later he began an independent study of God's Word and produced his important apology for the Bible, entitled *Truth of Scripture*. Still later came his treatise *On the Church* which had such a wide influence on Bohemia and led to the rise of the Hussites there. Wycliffe's theology held that the church is a fellowship made up of the saved; consequently, no one can be head of the Church but Christ Himself. Believing laymen, he held, have Christ as their priest, shepherd, bishop and pope. From 1378, until his death in 1384, he carried on a struggle with the Church's hierarchy in Britain. He was driven from Oxford to a rural parish where he and his associates completed the first major English translation of the Bible. One of the main reasons Wycliffe translated the Bible was to enable church leaders to read the Scriptures and then restore the church to its original functions described in the New Testament. He contended that it was the sacred privilege and right of Christians in all ages to examine the current manifestations of the Church, evaluate them by Holy Scripture, and restore the true faith of the Apostolic Church. The Lollards, with whom Wycliffe was not directly connected, accepted his views and became the channel through which they were widely and popularly disseminated. In 1409 an act was promulgated prohibiting all preaching outside the Roman churches. All the writings of Wycliffe were ordered destroyed. There was a great bonfire at Lutterworth including Wycliffe's books and papers and his remains dug up from the grave. The ashes of all were committed to the Thames as State and Church authorities looked on in unholy glee. The free churches went underground to reappear in the Puritan movement in 1560.

As the Roman Church moved to suppress the free church idea in England, the movement inspired by Wycliffe in Bohemia developed in a powerful way. John Huss,[15] professor at the University of Prague and pastor of the influential Bethlehem Church there, began preaching the pure Christian faith of the New Testament and calling upon the Church of Rome to repent and return to that faith. Unfortunately Hussism was later identified with a strong Czech anti-German nationalist political movement which called for an open break with Rome.

Church and State authorities combined in demanding that Huss cease his preaching. When he refused he was burned at the stake in July, 1415. Again the free churches went underground to emerge in 1467 as the United Brethren *(Unitas Fratrum)*. This group selected its own pastors and used the title "bishop" for the outstanding leader of the fellowship. Back of the formation of the United Brethren was Peter Cheltschizki who persuaded his people to accept the doctrine of separation of Church and State. Lucas of Prague, his successor, led the Bohemian Brethren in the promotion of individual Bible reading and fellowship in conventicles and free churches. In Bohemian regions where the Waldensians were strong and where the Anabaptists later developed there was a fine spirit of intercommunion as the Church of the New Testament began to grow in numbers and influence.

So concerned were the "powers that be" in Rome about the continuing free Church that they had counsel together and brought into being a new institution known as the Inquisition.[16] Pope Gregory IX proclaimed that all Christians who refused to acknowledge the authority of Rome be examined as to the validity of their faith. The standards of judgment were to be the decrees of the Church Councils at Toulouse, Tours, Verona and Lateran. Judges were delegated to act in Gregory's name and pronounce judgment on all who refused to recant. Defendants were tried in secret and not allowed legal advisors or witnesses. Tortures of various sorts were applied until confessions of guilt were secured. Punishments took the form of fasts, prayers, flagellations, pilgrimages, crosses sewn on the flesh and imprisonment under unsanitary conditions. The property of suspects was confiscated by the Church. It proved profitable to the Inquisition to prosecute the dead whose estates lay in legal jeopardy for as long as forty years. The judges came mainly from the Dominican Order. The trials began first in Lombardy and spread into all sections of Western Europe save England and Scandanavia. Northern Italy, Southern France and Northern Spain were visited with fiendish thoroughness. Indeed, the Spanish Inquisition has become a synonym for horror in the English language.

But even this strategy of the imperial Catholic Church could not kill the Apostolic free church. The blood of martyrs became the seed of Christian freedom.

In the early days of the sixteenth century God raised up Martin Luther[17] in Germany to stay the march of Rome. Trained in a monastery and attaining the doctorate, he devoted himself to a study of the Bible in which he found freedom from scholastic theology, the dogmatic authority of Rome with its hierarchy and traditions, the power of prejudice and every human ordinance. He desired to impart this freedom to all men. Since he learned it from the Scriptures, he knew that the best way to promote freedom was to make the Bible available for the widest possible reading and study. After years of laborious effort he completed his translation of the Bible into the German vernacular and made thousands of copies available. This accomplishment alone put into the hands of free churchmen and sincere seekers after the Truth as it is in Christ Jesus, the means by which a tidal wave of religious freedom rose to sweep the world.

In the earlier days of Luther's attempt to stay the march of Roman Catholicism, he adhered rather faithfully to the principle of *sola scriptura*. This led him to defy the pope, abolish the mass, teach the principle of justification by faith, abrogate the celibacy of the clergy, restore the preaching office, and discard compulsory fasts and many other distinctly Roman practices. At one time he favored the practice of immersion and congregational polity, but political, nationalistic and economic pressures eventually conspired to halt the free church movement so nobly begun and led him to accept the principle of union of Church and State and a species of hierarchial control of the churches.

The Anabaptist free church movement[18] arose in the same general area of Europe at about the same time. The aberrations of the Anabaptists must, of course, be condemned; but the movement as a whole contributed much to the restoration of the New Testament Church. Its passion was to discover from the pages of Holy Writ the pattern of the church of the first century and to renew original Christianity in doctrine, ordinances and life. Anabaptist leaders took Luther's Bible and made it their constant companion and guide. Haled into court by their persecutors, the Anabaptist knowledge of the Scriptures was more than a match for both Catholic and Reformed theologians. As Thomas van Imbroich stood in the court in Cologne about 1556, he declared, "The Scripture cannot be broken, nor shall anything be added to or subtracted from the Word of God which remains in eternity." Dirk Phillips wrote in his *Vindication:* "From these words it is evident that whatever God has not commanded and has not instituted by express command of Scripture, He does not want to be observed nor does He want to be served therewith, nor will He have His Word set aside nor made to suit the pleasure of men." The Anabaptists had a clear discernment of the relative importance of the New Testament over the Old Testament, and insisted that all doctrine and practice in the Church have New Testament support. Pilgrim Marpech compiled a book of more than 800 pages on the theme of Old and New Testament contrasts. Dirk Phillips pointed out that "the false prophets cover and disguise their deceptive doctrines by appealing to the letter of the Old Testament consisting of types and shadows. For whatever they cannot defend from the New Testament Scriptures they try to establish by the Old Testament . . . and this has given rise to many sects and to many false religious forms." Anabaptists opposed infant baptism, insisted on the rebaptism of knowledgeable adults and their preference for immersion resulted in their nickname. They preferred to be known as "brethren in Christ." They recognized no extra-congregational bishops. Their services were simple with great emphasis on the Lord's Supper and the fellowship exhibiting love, peace and goodwill to all men. They insisted on personal holiness and evidence of the new birth in daily living, rejecting completely the institutional concept of salvation common to Roman Catholicism and to the major churches of the Reformation. Luther, Zwingli, and Calvin used all their political power, of which they acquired much, to destroy the Anabaptist movement and succeeded to a tragic degree. There were stake burnings and executions which matched the worst that Rome had done. Anabaptists find their continuity to our day in the American Mennonites, but more especially in the Holland branch of that movement which gave strong support to English free church developments in the late sixteenth century.

When the Reformation came to England in the days of Henry VIII and Cranmer, the State Church continued to dominate the religious scene. However, many staunch evangelicals remained in England, conducted conventicles and worship services in secret. These free church Christians, remnants of the Lollard and Puritan movements, were determined not to submit to Romish tyranny. The Puritan opposition to the restructured Anglican Church grew in intensity until Roman Catholic Queen ("Bloody") Mary drove hundreds of them to Holland. During and following the reign of Queen Elizabeth I the free churches prospered anew, despite the disfavor of the State Church. In the 1580's Congregationalism appeared led by Robert Browne and others.[19] Browne was a graduate of Cambridge and was a man of high intellectual attainments. He organized the first church in Norwich in 1581 and was the author of the notable book, *A Treatise of Reformation Without Tarrying for Anie*, in which he advised all those who desired a free church after the New Testament pattern to leave the Established Church. Alongside the "Brownites" Baptist congregations developed, some of which claimed unbroken relations with free churches founded as early as 1580. There was often close cooperation between the Puritans, Congregationalists and Baptists, driven as they often were to unitedly defend their very right to exist in England. The Puritan movement reached its peak under Cromwell the Great, but after his fall, because of certain political connotations, it suffered new lows. The struggle with the Stuarts, and especially Archbishop Laud, eventuated in the migration to America. It was in the "New World" that the free church had its great opportunity.[20] There were no domineering church organizations demanding subservience and thousands of immigrants built their own church bodies according to their own convictions. The romantic voyage of the *Mayflower* in 1620 brought the first important English Puritan refugees from Holland.[21] The churches emanating from the Plymouth colony were all free church in polity and formed what we know as the Congregational Churches of America. They were followed by the Baptist pioneers who in Rhode Island in 1638 founded what proved to be the largest Protestant body in North America. Baptists were free church men and zealously insisted upon reproducing churches after the simple New Testament pattern. Quakers, who had their origin in England in the work of George Fox (1624-1691), came to America in 1662 under the leadership of William Penn, the founder of Pennsylvania. They too were free church in polity and might be said to be almost "extremists" in their emphasis on simplicity in church organization. Out of this tremendous complex of free churches came a new day in Protestantism and the spirit which has made the United States of America the greatest Protestant-oriented nation in the world.

But in this treatise we have special interest in the free church backgrounds from which came the early leaders of the people known as "Disciples of Christ." In Scotland in the 1700s, the Haldane brothers[22] were raised up for a great free church testimony. Robert Richardson, in his *Memoirs of Alexander Campbell*,[23] devotes two chapters to the Haldane movement which he credits with giving Alexander Campbell "his first impulse as a religious reformer, and which may be justly regarded as the *first phase* of the religious reformation which he carried out so successfully to its legitimate issues."

Robert and James A. Haldane were of distinguished Scottish ancestry and sons of a very pious mother. Robert, the older brother, entered the Royal Navy and served with unusual distinction, retiring at length to a fine estate. Here his early impressions revived under the Spirit of God and he began a daily study of the Holy Scriptures. Though devoted to the kirk, he attributed to a lowly stonemason his first clear concepts of "the important truth that faith must cast away all reliance on frames and feelings and only rest on Christ." His full surrender to the Lord led him to dedicate all his time and his immense wealth to Christian pursuits.

James Haldane was not stirred as was his brother until, while attending the General Assembly of the Church of Scotland, he heard the discussions which eventuated in an adverse vote on a resolution, "That it is the duty of Christians to send the gospel to the heathen world." He was so sensitized by this exhibition of smug self-righteousness and lack of concern for the unsaved that he joined his brother in studying the Bible "in a childlike spirit, without seeking any interpretation that would agree with his own ideas." Both brothers were strongly attached to each other and agreed in the religious changes which their Bible study led them to make.

Having heard of the coldness and immorality among the clergy in northern Scotland, they set out in 1797 to distribute Bibles and tracts and hold open-air meetings in which they taught the Word of God. They based their right to preach "upon the indispensable duty of every Christian to warn sinners to flee from the wrath to come, and to point out Jesus as the way, the truth and the life." The State Church opposed them but the populace followed them with large audiences. Their activities came to the attention of the celebrated independent evangelist, Rowland Hill, whom they at length commissioned to open services in the great Circus of Edinburgh. This move caused tremendous religious excitement: as many as fifteen to twenty thousand persons attended the meetings. Thrilled by the responses of the people to the simple gospel, Robert Haldane proceeded at his own expense to erect tabernacles in the chief cities and towns of Scotland and to provide preachers. Not desiring to start a new denomination, it was agreed among the Haldanes and their co-laborers to associate themselves with the Congregationalists of England. James A. Haldane became the minister of the church in Edinburgh; Greville Ewing, in Glasgow. It was Ewing who became such a profound influence in the life of Alexander Campbell. Robert Haldane preferred to travel, covering Scotland many times, encouraging brethren of like faith in Bible study and good works. The most interesting of his journeys took him to Switzerland where he conducted Bible classes, chiefly in Geneva. Among the young men he inspired to lives of Christian service were Merle D'Aubignes, the historian of the Reformation; M. Malan, the hymn writer; F. Monod; Henri Pytt, and Felix Neff

Taking the Bible and the Bible alone as their rule of faith and practice, the Haldanes and their associates came to grave decisions involving not only a break with the Church of Scotland but also with the Congregationalists. Naturally these decisions had far-reaching consequences and led to divisions in the Haldane movement. However, the brothers had never sought to establish a denomination and viewed many of these changes in local church fellowship as normal results in a free search for Scriptural truth. Among the radical decisions made by the Haldanes was the rejection of all extra-congregational church government. They came to teach that Christ was the sole head of the Church and that local church government should be vested in a plurality of elders. Abandoning the doctrine of infant baptism, they eventually decided that only immersion of believers was sustained by the Scriptures. They early introduced the practice of every Sunday observance of the Lord's Supper and of weekly meetings for social worship in which all members were allowed to participate with prayers and testimonies. They were strongly insistent upon the necessity of a pious life by all professors of religion, and frequently resorted to strict disciplinary measures in their congregations.

The Haldane movement disappeared with the lengthening of the years, except for its somewhat nebulous relationship with the Plymouth Brethren and its spiritual kinship to the great Restoration Movement in America, but its influence will live forever.

The Free Church tradition is a thrilling one. To it we owe many of our modern blessings of religious liberty, civil freedom, and our basic concepts of justice in the English-speaking world. The measure of democratic and autonomous church government which is enjoyed in the institutionalized and catholicized denominations of our day is largely the result of the courageous stand of free churchmen in their centuries-old battle for their rights against the strongly entrenched political powers of ecclesiastical conformity.

Chapter V

THE CHOICE ON THE FRONTIER

O N the Appalachian frontier in the early days of the nineteenth
century was born the largest free church movement of distinctly
American origins. From small beginnings it has grown to embrace
over five million communicants.[1]

Church historians have credited these beginnings to the leadership
of Thomas and Alexander Campbell in Pennsylvania, Ohio and Vir-
ginia; to Barton W. Stone in Kentucky and the Ohio River valley;
to Abner Jones in New England; and James O'Kelley in the Carolinas. Jones and O'Kelley were neither by theological nor affinitive
nature *en rapport* with the Movement "to restore the New Testament
Church in doctrine, ordinances and life." Jones and his followers were
basically Unitarian in their views and the O'Kelleyites never got far
from their Wesleyan Methodist background. We shall, therefore, for
the purposes of this chapter, confine our study to the Campbell and
Stone movements which finally coalesced[2] into the communion known
as "Disciples of Christ."

There were three types of church polity already on the frontier when
the Campbells, and Stone, arrived — episcopal, presbyterial and congregational. In the episcopal system much of the Catholic tradition
survived. The Church was accented to prime importance and extra-
congregational bishops ruled over the clergy and the churches. A
monarchial hierarchy existed with elaborate clerical orders and local

churches had very little freedom of thought or action. The two major denominations on the frontier that accepted this form of church government were the Episcopal Church and the Methodist Episcopal Church. In the presbyterial system authority was vested in a series of extra-congregational assemblies: the general assembly at the national level, the synod at the state or regional level, and the presbytery in a prescribed district level. The local church had a session which, under normal conditions, governed in all congregational matters, but it was subject to the actions and directions of the superior assemblies. Denominations of the Presbyterian and Reformed tradition were strong on the frontier. And, then, there were the congregational-type churches such as the Baptist and Congregational that were growing rapidly in many parts of Appalachia. The free church polity of these last named denominations had a strong appeal to the pioneers who were advocates of free enterprise in a free state and who were bent on carving out of the wilderness a free society in which their posterity might enjoy "life, liberty and the pursuit of happiness." The Campbells and Stone were Presbyterians when they began their ministry on the frontier and as well-educated, cultured gentlemen were thoroughly conversant with all phases of the question of ecclesiastical polity and thoroughly capable of making a wise and well-considered choice of the form of church government which should obtain in the churches they served.

Thomas Campbell[3] was born in County Down, Ireland, February 1, 1763. His father was a strict member of the Church of England, but Thomas was never happy in the Anglican faith and was early in his life attracted to the Covenanter and Seceder Presbyterians. He eventually decided to become a Presbyterian minister. He received his ministerial education in Glasgow University and the Divinity Hall of that branch of the Secession known as the Anti-Burghers. The Scotch Presbyterians were in a continual turmoil over theological and political questions, much to the torture of Thomas Campbell's soul, and after a highly honorable ministry at Ahorey, broken in health, he sought to begin a new life in America.

But if Campbell thought to escape Presbyterian disunity in his new surroundings, he was mistaken. He was forced to enroll with the Anti-Burgher Synod of North America and was assigned to the Presbytery of Chartiers in Pennsylvania. He had not been there long until he committed the grievous error of offering communion to other kinds of Presbyterians and, to make a long story short, was unfrocked. Campbell, with about twenty of his friends, was now greatly burdened with the sadly divided state of Christendom, and organized the Christian Association of Washington, Pennsylvania, for the purpose of bearing a testimony to the Christian world in behalf of a united church. They were of various denominational persuasions and made it clear that they were not forming a new ecclesiastical body. One of the first things they did was to issue a document prepared by Campbell which has been hailed by scholars as the first great ecumenical pronouncement in American church history. It was entitled, *Declaration and Address*, and became for the Restoration Movement what the Declaration of Independence was for the United States of America.

The *Declaration and Address*[4] is of interest in our study primarily for its implications regarding church government. It was addressed "To all that love our Lord Jesus Christ in sincerity, throughout all the churches. . . Dearly Beloved Brethren." In this statement Campbell recognized the existence of the true universal spiritual body, the Church, and the supreme Headship of Jesus Christ in His Church. In his first "Proposition," Campbell said, "The church of Christ upon earth is essentially, intentionally, and constitutionally one; consisting of all those in every place that profess their faith in Christ and obedience to him in all things according to the Scriptures, and that manifest the same by their tempers and conduct, and of none else, as none else can be truly and properly called Christians." He goes on in "Proposition Two" to say, "Although the church of Christ upon earth must necessarily exist in particular and distinct societies, locally separate one from another; yet there ought to be no schisms, no uncharitable divisions among them. . ." And in "Proposition Five": "With respect to the commands and ordinances of our Lord Jesus Christ, where the Scriptures are silent, as to the express time or manner of performance, if any such there be; no human authority has power to interfere, in order to supply the supposed deficiency, by making laws for the church; nor can anything more be required of Christians in such cases, but only that they so observe these commands and ordinances, as will evidently answer the declared and obvious end of their institution. Much less has any human authority power to impose new commands or ordinances upon the church, which our Lord Jesus Christ has not enjoined. Nothing ought to be received into the faith or worship of the church; or be made a term of communion among Christians, that is not as old as the New Testament." In the main body of the document, as also in the *Appendix*, there is repeated emphasis on the definitive authority of the New Testament in all matters pertaining to the Church. It is small wonder that, building on the basic principles of the *Declaration and Address*, the churches that were inspired by it became congregational free churches.

When Alexander Campbell, the son of Thomas, arrived in America and read his father's treatise, he gave it his full and complete endorsement. Alexander, too, was a product of Glasgow University and was an Anti-Burgher Presbyterian, but he had been deeply impressed by the ministry of the noted independent evangelist, Rowland Hill.

Hill had visited Rich Hill, an Independent church near Ahorey, for their first encounter. This congregation was connected with the Puritan movement in England, and its pulpit was frequently filled by Alexander Carson, John Walker and James Alexander Haldane. The Rich Hill Independents observed the Lord's Supper in the "evangelical style," and reflected in many ways an earnestness and zeal for the salvation of souls. Greville Ewing, the popular and scholarly minister of the great Haldane tabernacle in Glasgow, formed a strong attachment for young Campbell, inviting him to his home for discussions on religion and for social gatherings. Contrasting the Independent freedom of thought and action, within the limits of Scriptural authority, with the spiritual despotism and denominational prejudice of the right-wing Presbyterianism of his day, Campbell was moved to consider seriously the claims of independency.[5]

With this background Alexander was providentially conditioned to sacrificially and zealously associate himself with his father in the common objective to "restore the New Testament Church in doctrine, ordinances and life" in order that the Church on earth might be one. They believed that this could be accomplished only by an appeal to "the

Bible and the Bible alone as the authoritative rule of faith and practice" and through churches free to accept their findings.

Deprived of the blessings of fellowship in any duly constituted church, the Campbells in the spring of 1811 came to feel the Christian Association must become an independent church. Accordingly, in a community building near Mount Pleasant, Pennsylvania, the group constituted itself into a local church, congregational in form of government. Thomas Campbell was chosen elder, and his son Alexander was licensed to preach the Gospel. William Gilchrist then offered a site for the construction of a new meeting house. A simple frame structure was erected at Brush Run and the congregation sought to develop a local church after the New Testament pattern.[6]

It regarded neighboring religious bodies as possessing the substance of Christianity, but as having failed to preserve "the form of sound words" in which it was originally presented.

The abandonment of every human system and a return to the Bible and the Bible alone as the rule of faith and practice were its chief objectives.

It regarded each local church as an independent organization, having its own local government by bishops and deacons, yet not so absolutely independent of other churches as not to be bound to them by fraternal relations.

In function the congregation ministered to the sick and needy, was evangelistic, gave itself to teaching and preaching, provided "the breaking of bread and the prayers," and promoted Christian fellowship.

Considering "lay preaching" as authorized, it denied the distinction between clergy and laity to be Scriptural.

It observed the Lord's Supper every Lord's Day.

Receiving no doctrine but that which was expressly revealed, it was prepared to abandon many things considered precious and important in the traditional churches around them.

Paying no respect whatever to the theological and ecclesiastical controversies which had raged in the churches since the times of the Apostles, it proposed to restudy the Scriptures to discover the foundation and structure of the New Testament Church and restore its entire form and spirit on the new frontier. This was all by deliberate choice. The Brush Run brethren preferred this kind of church to the other kinds they knew. They took no counsel from their cultural, social, psychological, or economic needs. They were determined to know no doctrine, polity, or practice, but that revealed in the New Testament. From then on to the end of time they and their posterity would be a people completely committed to the New Testament way.

On July 4, 1823, Alexander Campbell issued the first number of a new periodical, *The Christian Baptist*. In his preface he wrote: "We expect to prove whether a paper perfectly independent, free from any controlling jurisdiction except the Bible, will be read; or whether it will be blasted by the poisonous breath of sectarian zeal and of an aspiring priesthood." The leading article was a brief review of the Christian religion as first established, showing the prophetic background of the Messiah, His lowly advent and His glorious victory in the atonement as the suffering Saviour. Campbell dwelt on the perfection of His teaching; the life and conduct of His disciples and of the Apostles; and contrasted them with modern religious teachers. He then described the New Testament churches as to their unity, their faith and love of Christ, their independence as local congregations, and their devotion to good works. By contrast, he presented a scathing picture of modern Christianity, its corruptions and divisions. This article became a pattern for the content of future issues. In an ensuing series on "The Restoration of the Ancient Order of Things," he plead for the abandonment of everything not in use by the early Christians and the adoption of everything sanctioned by primitive practice. He stressed the independence of each local church under a plurality of bishops (elders) and deacons. He called for the overthrow of all extra-congregational clerical and ecclesiastical power.

Both Alexander and his father sought in every way possible to avoid setting up a new denominational structure. They turned to the Baptists as a people nearest the New Testament doctrine and practice, and the growing number of independent churches of Christ joined the Baptist Associations already in existence. But it was not long until differences arose. Finally the Beaver (Pennsylvania) Association of Regular Baptists issued the historic "Beaver Anathema" against doctrines of the Campbells and their associates. This was the beginning of the end of a beautiful friendship. The Campbells and Walter Scott, its evangelist, were members of the Mahoning (Ohio) Association which was controlled by the free churches. At its Austintown meeting in 1830, there was a deep undercurrent of conviction that all extra-congregational agencies were unscriptural and a source of trouble. John Henry, at the instigation of Walter Scott, offered a resolution that the Association, as an advisory council, be dissolved at once.[7] Almost without debate, the resolution passed and the Mahoning Association adjourned *sine die*. Thereafter for many years there were no extra-congregational assemblies of the free churches of Christ, except "Yearly Meetings"— purely voluntary, non-corporative gatherings for fellowship and Gospel preaching. As the years passed these mass meetings grew in size and enthusiasm sometimes attaining an attendance of as high as five thousand.

Alexander Campbell himself was not too well pleased with what happened at Austintown. He later confessed that he was alarmed "at the impassioned and hasty manner in which the Association was, in a few minutes, dissolved" and counselled "occasional, if not stated, deliberative meetings on questions of expediency. . ." in the future development of the movement. In a later chapter we shall consider his maturer views on extra-congregational association and co-operation. But out on the frontier in their early days Disciples of Christ were free churchmen of the deepest dye.

Now for a look at the Kentucky phase of the Movement under the leadership of Barton W. Stone.[8] Stone was a Presbyterian educated for the ministry in the famous David Caldwell Academy, near Greensboro, North Carolina, where nearly all Carolina Presbyterian preachers of status and stature were trained in the late 1700s. In 1798 Stone was called to the stated ministry of the Presbyterian churches at Cane Ridge and Concord, in the Transylvania Presbytery (Kentucky). Strongly influenced by the Great Awakening, a highly emotional religious revival that was sweeping the frontier, he was led to "advance the Redeemer's Kingdom without regard to religious parties." After six years as a Presbyterian pastor at Concord and Cane Ridge, Stone dramatically called his congregations together and informed them that he "could no longer conscientiously preach to support the Presbyterian Church."

Stone had come to know the importance and the joy of a personal Christian experience. He now believed it was possible for the Holy Spirit to enlighten and guide men in the study of the Word of God apart from the traditional creeds and ecclesiastical paraphernalia of Christendom. He saw the sinfulness of division in the body of Christ. He shared in the democratic liberty of the frontier and was completely disillusioned about the values of extra-congregational ecclesiastical authority. He had found in the Great Awakening a demonstration of Christian unity among men of a common Christian faith, and he was ready to mount a great spiritual crusade for the restoration of the Church as it was in the days of the Apostles.

Stone's close associates in the "Revival Movement" faced similar decisions as to their status in the Presbyterian denomination. They finally, as a body, renounced the jurisdiction of the Presbyterian Synod of Kentucky and in 1803 formed the independent Springfield Presbytery.[9] This organization survived only nine months. Its creators soon saw that it could become as dangerous a source of tyranny as the ecclesiasticism they had just abandoned. So on June 28, 1804, they issued at Cane Ridge *The Last Will and Testament of the Springfield Presbytery*,[10] a document highly revered in the archives of the Restoration Movement. We quote from the first half, which has special relevance to church polity:

"The Presbytery of Springfield, sitting at Cane Ridge, in the county of Bourbon, being, through a gracious Providence, in more than ordinary bodily health, growing in strength and size daily; and in perfect soundness and composure of mind; and knowing that it is appointed for all delegated bodies once to die; and considering that the life of every such body is very uncertain, do make and ordain this our last Will and Testament, in manner and form following, viz:

"*Imprimis.* We *will*, that this body die, be dissolved, and sink into union with the Body of Christ at large; for there is but one body, and one Spirit, even as we are called in one hope of our calling.

"*Item*. We *will*, that our name of distinction, with its Reverend title, be forgotten, that there be but one Lord over God's heritage and his name one.

"*Item*. We *will*, that our power of making laws for the government of the church, and executing them by delegated authority, forever cease; that the people may have free course to the Bible, and adopt the *law of the Spirit of life in Christ Jesus*.

"*Item*. We *will*, that candidates for the Gospel ministry henceforth study the Holy Scriptures with fervent prayer, and obtain license from God, to preach the simple Gospel, with the Holy Ghost sent down from heaven, without any mixture of philosophy, vain deceit, traditions of men or the rudiments of this world. And let none henceforth take this honor to himself, but he that is called of God, as was Aaron.

"*Item*. We *will*, that the church of Christ resume her native right of internal government—try her candidates for the ministry, as to the soundness of their faith, acquaintance with experimental religion, gravity and aptness to teach; and admit no other proof of their authority but Christ speaking in them. We will, that the church of Christ look to the Lord of the harvest to send forth laborers into his harvest; and that she resume her primitive right of trying those who say they are apostles, and are not.

"*Item*. We *will*, that each particular church, as a body, actuated by the same spirit, choose her own preacher, and support him by freewill offering, without a written call or subscription, admit members, remove offenses; and never henceforth delegate her right of government to any man or set of men whatever. . ."

The *Last Will and Testament* in its published form included an "Address" which reiterated the opposition of the witnesses, who attested it, to "church sessions, presbyteries, synods, general assemblies, etc." as without precedent in the New Testament and closed with an appeal for the unity of all believers.

While no authentic figures are available it is estimated by 1830 there were some fifteen thousand "Christians only" in these free churches that multiplied in Kentucky and the Ohio River valley after this bold break with Presbyterianism.

Other like-minded groups associated themselves with the Stone movement, such as the Scotch Baptists who preferred the name "Church of Christ" for their congregations, and some Regular Baptists who had been influenced by reading Alexander Campbell's *Christian Baptist*. Immigration from the Carolinas brought some "Republican Methodists" into Kentucky. They naturally coalesced with the "Christians." Their Wesleyan background was reflected in a Conference-type polity which they introduced into the brotherhood, but which completely disappeared when these churches withdrew to form a separate denomination with headquarters at Dayton, Ohio.

The strict adherence of the Stone movement to free-church polity was significantly demonstrated in the union which took place with the Campbell movement in 1831-32.[11] Campbell met Stone for the first time when he visited Kentucky in 1824. The two men at once formed a warm personal attachment to each other, which was to continue through life. They recognized the fact that they were engaged in identical ministries with the same general objectives. Thereupon ensued an immense correspondence through which it was concluded that the two movements ought to be merged into one. There were, however, no extra-congregational authoritative ecclesiastical bodies through which such a union might be negotiated, validated and consummated. Historians have fixed the date and place of union as October 16, 1831, at Lexington, Kentucky. This event, however, was simply a voluntary gathering of ministers and other brethren from the two communions (Campbell was not present) who, under an outpouring of the Holy Spirit, pledged to Christ and to one another their own abiding fellowship in one body, and who confessed to an overwhelming faith that all their brethren everywhere would embrace one another in an enduring union. Stone, who was present and strangely stirred by the conviction that this was the work of God, wrote in the next issue of his magazine, *Christian Messenger*, "They were united by no written compact, no conventional constitution. . . They were free to think for themselves without the dictation of ghostly bishops . . . were drawn together by the spirit of truth as taught by our common Lord and experienced by us, the subjects of his kingdom." After Lexington, individual ministers took to horseback, contacting the ministers and elders of local churches, meeting with brethren in union assemblies, spreading brotherly love, and stimulating commitments to a united testimony. No more inspiring ecumenical accomplishment has been recorded in the pages of American church history than this union of free churches in the Providence of God.

The unanimous, voluntary, intelligent choice of a free church, congregational polity by Disciples of Christ on the Appalachian frontier has been validated in accepted practice for over 150 years. To surrender this freedom for the sake of a return, in the name of ecumenicity, to the polities our fathers rejected, or to some synthesis or compromise of such unscriptural human expediencies, would be a step backward from the advanced ground Disciples of Christ have so long held in the company of those who love the Lord.

Chapter VI

INDIVIDUAL FREEDOM

THE Free Church puts a premium on the individual. It has a unique awareness of two facts: (1) without individual members there can be no body, and (2) the power of the Church lies in saved men personally linked with Christ.

Out on the Appalachian frontier this concept was demonstrated in many ways: preachers frequently warned against the dangers of "joining the church," in the sense that their denominational neighbors used the phrase. They said, saved men become members of Christ's body and because of that relationship are automatically members of the Church. . . This relationship was emphasized in the simple creedal requirement—complete personal commitment to the living Christ. When people came forward in the assembly to accept Christ as their Saviour, they were asked to make the simple confession, "I believe that Jesus is the Christ, the Son of God and my *personal* Saviour." Repentant believers were baptized "into Christ" and henceforth bore His name. . . The fathers were fond of quoting Revelation 1:6: "He hath made us kings and priests unto God. . .," and they acted as though they believed it. . . There were no "clergy" and "laity" in the churches. All were brethren in Christ. . . Church services made "the Lord's table" the center of worship. Often there was no preacher. The elders presided over what was called a "social service" in which individual Christians took part, according to "the Lord's leading," by

60

prayer, testimony or the calling of a hymn. . . During the week members went out "two by two" to win souls to Christ. . . Members carried their New Testaments with them wherever they went "searching the Scriptures daily" and sharing their faith with all they met. . . They were usually ready to "give a reason for the hope" that was within them. . . In formal worship services all the elders would frequently occupy the platform, one would lead the congregational singing, another would read the Scripture lesson, another offer prayer, another "lift the offering," others preside at the communion service, and the preaching elder would bring the discourse. There was no "priestly" or "pastoral" superiority manifest. All were equal before Christ discharging their individual functions to His glory. . . Each member felt a responsibility for "extending the kingdom." When opportunities opened for establishing new congregations in neighboring communities, individual members would without hesitancy offer their services for the task. . . When a family moved to another location where there was no "church after the New Testament pattern," they spread the communion table in their home, invited their neighbors to worship with them and soon had the nucleus of a new congregation. . . Many intelligent business and professional men well versed in the Scriptures were also free-lance evangelists, held "protracted meetings" and "encouraged the brethren" in the weaker churches often without any financial remuneration.

As in the apostolic Church, the churches of Christ on the frontier expected each and every member to accept his or her responsibility in the body of Christ. Nowhere was there perceived to be a separation or even a distinction made between those who did and did not minister, between the active and passive members of the body, between those who gave and those who received; yet there existed in the *Ecclesia* a universal duty and a right of service, a universal readiness to serve and at the same time the widest possible varieties of functions. There was also, in a very real sense, the dependence of all kinds of ministers and ministrations on the One Lord. There was the Divine-human relationship and the man-to-man relationship, the vertical and the horizontal, but the individual was always involved.

It may be helpful to explore in some depth the reasons for the high degree of importance the Free Church attaches to the individual Christian and to his rights and privileges under God.

Item. The first reason has to do with the nature of man. Christianity considers man to be "made in the image of God" and not merely a rational animal. It recognizes his finite existence and his human weaknesses, but it also sees his capacity to transcend the natural world and his own self in response to the will of God. It knows his sinful nature but offers him redemption in Jesus Christ the Saviour. As "free in Christ" it enables him to grow into a life of noble values and ends, and into a happy realization of his highest and best hopes. Man is the supreme attainment of God's creation; linked in saving faith to Christ he is the answer to God's deepest longings. Man is worth the best that the Church can give.

Item. The Church is by nature the Body of Christ consisting of individual persons and of nothing but persons. They form a fellowship in Christ, and because of that relationship they are in fellowship with one another. This fellowship we call the Church does not exist independently in its own right; it flows from communion with Christ made real in the lives of the individual Christians who compose the fellowship. Therefore, the spiritual health of individual members of the Body must be of prime concern to the Church. If "one member suffers, all the members suffer with it; or (if) one member be honored, all the members rejoice with it. Now ye are the body of Christ, and members in particular," says the Apostle Paul in I Corinthians 12:26, 27.

Spiritual health involves the moral and spiritual growth of the individual Christian. The Apostle Paul urged "growth in grace and the knowledge of our Lord and Saviour Jesus Christ." And in writing to the Ephesians he proposed the startling goal that "all come to the unity of the faith, and of the knowledge of the Son of God, unto a perfect man, unto the measure of the stature of the fulness of Christ." It is the responsibility of the Church to provide the climate and the means by which each individual member can grow up in Christ to be reliable, honest, just, pure, tenderhearted, loving, merciful, patient, forgiving— reflecting in his life the characteristics which marked the life of Christ on earth.

Item. The chief business of the Church is the seeking and saving of lost and sinful men. There is no such thing as "social salvation." A man cannot be saved by "joining the church" or a society, or an institution. This is the lesson that Jesus tried to teach Nicodemus, a member of the Sanhedrin and, as such, committed to the concept of a Hebrew national righteousness. The Master told him, "Except *a man* be born of water and of the Spirit, *he* cannot enter into the kingdom of God" (John 3:5). And on the Day of Pentecost, Peter called for no mass conversions, but insisted, "Repent and be baptized *every one* of you. . ." (Acts 2:38), and you will receive the gift of the Holy Spirit. The whole history of salvation in the New Testament is a history of individual, personal encounter with the saving Christ. It is only through evangelistically committed and inspired individuals going out into the "highways and byways" and persuading other individuals to accept Christ as their Saviour that the Church will grow. The Church must be interested in persons or it will die.

Item. The church thrives on discipleship — an intensely individual and personal matter. Who is a disciple of Christ? He is one who is unwithholdingly committed to Christ, who denies himself daily, who takes up his cross and follows Him. Disciples are not to be confused with church members. Mere churchmen may live a divided life, a portion of it for self and a portion of it for Christ. The main trend of the true disciple's life is toward Christ and away from self, and his delight is in doing the will of his Lord. It is one of the provisions of divine grace that the self-denying Christian is the free man, the happy man in Christ. In the Free Church there are innumerable opportunities to serve Christ, unlimited chances of doing good, unlimited means of growth in knowledge of the truth, unlimited occasions for burden bearing and loving service. Personal loyalty to Jesus Christ and active participation in the work of His kingdom is the church's maximum incentive. To follow Him as the only Way, Truth and Life is the supreme stimulus to the full and free enjoyment of the Christian life; and to the release of the dynamic spiritual forces with which the church has been endowed. Those who would restructure Christian discipleship have worked out elaborate and exhaustive outlines of local church organization and administration, and of guidance for efficient discipleship. They issue from Headquarters great reams of analyses; firstlies, secondlies and thirdlies; tentative planning drafts; standards for measuring Christian stewardship, etc., etc., etc. There is abundant guidance for dramatics, worship programs, psychological and social analysis — all designed to interest church members in a more effective church program. But by no such dry and dusty techniques will men and women be inspired to do the work Christ has given His Church to accomplish. When the Christian discipleship described in the New Testament becomes the major thought and working principle in our churches, rather than mere church membership, we may expect the long-delayed spiritual revolution for which godly men and women are praying.

Item. The Free Church guarantees to the individual Christian the right and privilege to study the Holy Scriptures for himself and to explore the wonderful height, depth and breadth of God's revealed Truth contained therein. He is not bound by human creeds or dogmas enunciated by extra-congregational or superimposed human ecclesiastical authorities. The only thought in the world that is worth anything is free thought. Brains are a great misfortune if bishops or priests do not permit the followers of Christ to use them. It is out of the untrammeled freedom of thought exercised by free men in Christ that have come some of the greatest spiritual and ethical movements in history. The impact of fresh new facets of truth on the soul stimulates utterance and action, perforce resulting in Christian advance and progress. Said Carlyle, "A thinking man is the worst enemy the Prince of Darkness can have." Free churches are the only churches that dare encourage such a dangerous practice as studying and interpreting the Word of God for oneself under the guidance of the Holy Spirit.

A word of caution needs to be raised at this point: Individual freedom in churches of Christ is not a license for anarchy. The New Testament churches were conducted "in decency and in order." The eldership in particular was charged with the oversight, the guidance and the discipline of the flock. Discipline is a word that is seldom heard these days in the churches. Discipline, in the New Testament, includes instruction, training in "all things that pertain unto life and godliness" and correction in "righteousness." In case of willful recalcitrance or disorderly walk, it is the duty of the eldership to eliminate such persons from the fellowship. Discipline in the church involves such watch-care and training of its members as a parent should exercise over his children "bringing them up in the nurture and admonition of the Lord." Elders must "watch for their souls as they that must give an account, that they may do it with joy and not with grief." When offenses come, wise discipline will first seek to reform the offender by admonition, exhortation, reproof and rebuke. If these fail, more stringent action is needed. All discipline should be exercised in the spirit of Christ with wisdom and discrimination. There is no such thing in a church of Christ as freedom to say and do those things which are not in harmony with the will of Christ or with the guidance of the Holy Spirit revealed in the Scriptures.

But what is the prospect for this concept of the preferred place of the individual in the churches, in today's and tomorrow's world? In every phase of modern life there is a trend toward socialization, institutionalization and away from individual rights and freedoms. There is increasing emphasis on the responsibility of the Church in building a better world; indeed, in some quarters, this obligation is stressed to the elimination of the basic functions of the Church described in the New Testament.

There is nothing new about this idea of social or institutional salvation. The Old Testament is filled with it. In the earlier stages of the Hebrew religion, in what Alexander Campbell called the "Starlight Age," righteousness was considered a tribal matter.[1] Then came a day, in the "Moonlight Age," when the tribes amalgamated into a nation and the individual had virtually no religious existence apart from the nation. The nation was the religious, as well as the political unit, and through the Old Testament, the nation was spoken of as though it were an individual. Through hundreds of years the religious thinking of the Jews was done in a nationalistic frame of reference. Its leaders too often considered the security of "The Chosen People" to be the nation's warriors, its spears, its horses and its chariots. But in the eighth century before Christ came a cataclysmic change in the life of Israel. Ten of the tribes of the nation were carried off into Assyrian captivity and they never came back. In the sixth century the two other tribes were driven in Babylonian captivity, and the City of God—the great Jerusalem—and the Temple were burned. Social righteousness suffered a blow from which the Hebrew people have never fully recovered. It was while the remnant of the two tribes was enslaved in Babylon that there came a return to individual righteousness as the essence of the true religion. People met in their slave quarters—the more fortunate in their homes—and worshipped God as individuals. Then came the synagogue[2] idea, so much of which is to be found in the New Testament Church of Christ, in which free companies of believers in Jehovah prayed together, studied the Law together, and sought to honor God with their daily lives and testimonies. They resolutely refused to be influenced or guided by the pagan mores of the Babylonians. Individual commitment to God and the free association of believers in synagogue worship were the only survival values of a once great corporate religion. Despite this testimony of the Old Testament Scriptures, many modern so-called "Christian" leaders are insisting on a return to the hollow and discredited formalisms of Hebrew institutional religion.

The Apostle Paul, an erudite scholar in Hebrew law and history, must have had this ancient debacle in mind when he wrote his letter to the Church of Christ in Rome. Rome was the center of the social and political power that ruled the whole known world. What should be the strategy of the Church, persecuted and terrorized on every hand, in this Great Society? The Apostle, after describing the wickedness and degradation of the Roman social order and reiterating his faith in the power of the Gospel, said, in Romans 12:1, 2: "I beseech you therefore, brethren, by the power of God, that ye present your bodies a living sacrifice, holy, acceptable to God, which is your reasonable service. And be not conformed to this world: but be ye transformed by the renewing of your mind, that ye may prove (demonstrate) what is that good, and acceptable, and perfect will of God." He moves on, in the twelfth chapter and most of the remaining chapters of this epistle, to describe the kind of individual Christian living that eventually, under God, was to change and transform the Roman world.

The effect of the Christian way of life upon that society is convincingly described[3] by Paul Monroe in his *History of Education:* "It is the unanimous testimony of historians that for the first two centuries, and for a large part of the third, the life upheld by the Christian church, with its purity yet unsullied and its ambitions yet untainted, furnished one of the most remarkable phenomena in history." Monroe goes on to describe what took place. "The gladiatorial shows, which had extended their demoralizing influence throughout the Empire, were put down by the Church, though not without a long struggle; divorce, which had become such an evil that it was said men changed their wives as easily as their clothes, was forbidden or strictly regulated; infanticide, which was universally practiced and had been largely responsible for the shrinkage of population and had been combated, when at all, by philosophers and government only on political grounds and hence ineffectively, was now opposed on moral grounds and rooted out of the Church, and finally out of society at large; in a similar manner, the exposure of children was definitely treated as murder, and through the teaching of the early Church and the large sums of money which it spent in the care of such children, was discontinued; the immoral ceremonies and the lascivious practices of private worship in the pagan religions were of course denied all the communicants of the new Church and in due time were driven from public tolerance. In these respects and, above all, through the high standard of personal morality, as expressed by the Mosaic Law and the Sermon on the Mount, standards altogether unknown among the masses of population, the early Church enforced a moral education that was entirely new in the history of the world and the history of education. If one will compare the simplicity and purity of the character of early Christian worship with the ceremonies of the pagan religions; the character of the Christian priesthood with that of the pagan cults; the morality inculcated in the one with the habit fostered in the other; the sacrifice entailed in the one with the cruelty and brutality, however refined, in the other; the charity and generosity of the one with the selfishness of the other; if these comparisons are made, the importance of Christianity will be readily understood." Thus was demonstrated the power of the individual, or, rather, the power of God working through consecrated Christian individuals.

But say the critics, we are living in a new age. William H. Whyte,

Jr., in his trenchant book, *The Organization Man,* contends[4] that there is no place in our modern collective society for individual freedom or individualistic beliefs. This is an age of the masses; the age of centralized organizational controls. Whyte says, in effect, that the businessman has disappeared, vanished into the corporation; the wage earner is gone, hidden in the union; the editor has faded out as a tool of the publishing house; the politician or statesman has "bleached out" in the party. And now come the modern Church leaders, mouthing the same doctrine, and saying, "The individual Christian must become lost in the Church." They accordingly propose to restructure the Church in such a way as to make Christians the creatures of a powerful institution; faceless people to be moved about on a world chessboard by the top men in a great hierarchy for the achievement of certain ecclesiastical, social and political goals.

The Free Church is the last best hope for individual freedom. It is the "City of Refuge" for those who still believe that they are individually made in the image of God, that He has need of them and can use them to accomplish His purposes in the Church and in the world. This belief is not *passe.* An illustration from science: The development of atomic energy has given new significance to the infinitesimal. The physics of a generation ago talked about potential and kinetic energy; the force exerted was calculated in terms of mass times velocity. One ton weight hoisted to the height of ten feet and dropped had great kinetic energy; but if you dropped a tiny portion of that weight, a pound, say, little energy was involved. But now, with our knowledge of atomic energy, we have learned to concentrate on the tiniest possible component of that one ton mass, the atom (so small that it cannot be seen), and release it to create astounding power. We now know that there is far more energy locked up in the individual atom than in the totality of atoms comprising the one ton weight dealt with *en masse.* The individual is discarded today by the sociologists and statesmen, the theologians and the ecclesiastics as a negligible force factor in power planning and is often condemned as an obstruction to the achievement of their purposes. The Free Church's evaluation of the individual eminently qualifies it to take full advantage of this tremendously potent force.

Did you ever study the parables of Jesus to discover how much He valued the individual? They are mostly organized around "a certain man," "a certain king," "a certain householder," "a certain rich man." He did not tell parables about races, or nations, or institutions. In them He focused our minds on the individual and, incidentally, upon ourselves. His teachings have a personal thrust that inspires personal commitment and action. It is thus He expects to accomplish His ultimate purposes.

Christ's own life is the supreme example of the premium God puts on the individual — He sent one person, His only begotten Son, and announced that belief in one God-man would give eternal life to all who would accept and obey Him. It is the message of the Christian religion that all the problems that vex, perplex and enslave humanity can be solved by the one, the only Jesus Christ.

What God has sanctified through His Son, let not the Church destroy!

Chapter VII

CONGREGATIONAL FREEDOM

THE pioneers of the Restoration Movement discovered by their study of the Holy Scriptures that a local church of Christ is a company of believers in Jesus Christ who have covenanted together to meet in a given place for public worship and to be governed in all things by the law of Christ. The rights and freedoms of this congregation are based on the rights and freedoms of the individual members of the Body of Christ who compose it. All are members on the same plane and enjoy a common fellowship. They are one in Christ. Because of the New Testament principle of the priesthood of all believers, they have equal rights and freedoms, but recognize the delegated authority of those whom they elect to rule over them. They retain equal rights to participate in an orderly way in all congregational acts. While recognizing other congregations as brethren in the universal Church of God and co-operating with them for the ongoing of the kingdom, the local church is independent and self-complete under Christ, the only true Head of the Church. Such, in essence, is the view expressed[1] by W. L. Hayden, in his *Church Polity*.

At the risk of being repetitive, our fathers discovered in Acts 6:5,6 that the local church has the right to choose its own servants; in Acts 11:22; 13:1-3; 14:26 that the local church may send out missionaries and evangelists; in II Corinthians 8:16-19, 23 that it may choose messengers for special purposes; in I Corinthians 5, and numerous other passages, that it can exercise discipline; in I Timothy 3 and Titus 1 that it should choose elders and deacons to lead the flock; in Acts 6:1-7 and I Timothy 5:9,16 that it should care for the needy. In all matters of discretion and expediency not specifically taught in the Word it was assumed by our fathers that the local congregation has the right to act, though not without regard to the basic principles of Christian belief and practice revealed in the New Testament. In matters of faith, piety and morality the local church was considered to be without authority. Supreme Church power, our fathers believed, is resident in Jesus Christ, its rightful and absolute ruler. His disciples are bound to do His will in all things revealed in the New Testament.

This concept of congregational freedom rules out the power of extra-congregational human authorities. It is not left in the power of any churchly superintendent, bishop, association or council, or any state in the world to add to, diminish, or alter the rights and freedoms of a local church given to it by God. This does not mean that local churches of Christ are free from all sense of responsibility to higher authority. They are acutely aware of being under the same authority as are all other churches of Christ, but this is a spiritual authority; it is that they will not accept any human authority imposed from without. It is not that they discard responsibility; it is that they reject any obligation to abide by decisions made for them by other religious agencies or organizations. It is not that they are opposed to order; it is that they refuse to regard themselves as subordinate units of some other ecclesiastical body which would control them in any matters whatsoever.

There is much being said these days about "restructuring" the Church in such a way as to preserve the rights of congregations and achieve "freedom with responsibility." The whole movement is external to the local churches and by its very nature seeks a species of extra-congregational control. It is important, therefore, that the churches have a clear and specific understanding of the extent of the freedoms which have been theirs for over 150 years.

Churches of Christ, after the New Testament pattern, are —

FREE to constitute themselves communions with God through Christ as independent, autonomous units, without the permission or approval of any human agency.

FREE to receive members according to the terms laid down by Christ and the apostles in the New Testament and to dismiss members who refuse to obey the rule of Christ.

FREE to choose and dismiss their own officers as provided in the New Testament without any outside authorization or approval.

FREE to call, ordain, retain and/or dismiss ministers without advice or approval from any extra-congregational body or ecclesiastical official. This right and privilege, however, must be exercised with deliberation, wisdom and caution while at the same time, by prayer and supplication, seeking the guidance of the Holy Spirit.

FREE to determine orders of worship and provide for the administration of the ordinances of Christ. Churches are not bound to accept liturgies, prayers, intercessions, observances of special days or any general method of conducting services provided by any extra-congregational agency. Indeed, to do so would tend to introduce a formalism into man's means of communication with God that could well destroy a spiritually meaningful and rewarding worship experience.

FREE to discipline their members in the "nurture and admonition of the Lord" provided that such discipline is exercised with wisdom, love and forbearance, according to the instruction of Holy Scripture.

FREE to provide all necessary means of teaching and training in the Word of God and to encourage Christian education in all its varied aspects. No outside agency has a right to determine the standards, methods or literature to be used in this process. While advantage should be taken of every reputable provision for the improvement of the quality of instruction and administration, great discrimination should be exercised in choices and uses.

FREE to make their own provisions for the needy of church and/or community in ways that seem best suited to the local situation. Many churches are now erecting their own children's home, rest homes, homes for the aged, welfare clinics and/or recreation centers. Where such substantial projects are impossible churches are free to support whatever good extra-congregational works they may choose.

FREE to send out their own missionaries and evangelists to seek and to save the lost in areas of their own choosing. They are at liberty to sponsor such workers and solicit aid in their support from other churches and individual Christians.

FREE to set up their own constitutions and by-laws and to make such rules of conduct or plans of work as may best serve their needs. Free exercise of initiative and creativity can assure maximum efficiency and progress. Offers of advisory assistance should be viewed with extreme caution lest they escalate into mandatory controls.

FREE to buy, build, maintain and dispose of property without the interference of any super-church or extra-congregational agency. They may and should reject all legal devices which would admit the rights of any district, state, area or national church body in such property.

FREE to manage their own finances. This involves the building of budgets, financial commitments from members, acceptance of steward-ship goals, support of church agencies and foreign advice in all fiscal matters. Lists of "approved" objects of support to the exclusion of others should be examined with extreme care in the light of their loyalty to the Word of God and the purposes to which the Church is com-mitted.

FREE to associate with whatever churches of like mind and heart they may choose, in the support of whatever undertakings they believe are for the advancement of Christ's kingdom, praying for the good and prosperity of all churches of Christ in all places and for their peace, increase in love and mutual edification.

FREE to participate in councils, rallies, conventions, lectureships, clinics and conferences, seeking ways and means of improving the effec-tiveness of the local church in its God-given tasks. In all such instances it should be understood that the churches are not bound by any decisions reached in such gatherings.

FREE to refrain from association in any or all such gatherings with-out being disfellowshipped as brethren in a common cause. This free-dom should also obtain in reverse, i.e., churches should not refuse to fellowship those that prefer to attend and work in such assemblies.

FREE to reject all attempts to impose upon them creeds, covenants, ministerial orders, programs, standards, goals or ecclesiastical structures for the sake of a specious "unity" or the achievement of "the wholeness of the Church."

FREE to refuse any patronage or control by the State, and to maintain strict separation of Church and State in all their activities.

FREE to maintain the highest possible standards in Church membership and in all relationships within and without their borders. Freedom is always ultimately justified by their ability to present to the community, to Christendom and to the world at large the best possible image of the true Church of Jesus Christ as it is revealed in the Holy Scriptures. If there is incompetence in leadership, if there is a low standard of life and fellowship, then no church polity however free can save the situation. Every individual congregation should be a center of spiritual power, and moral righteousness, a home of the saints, a servant to society, and an instrument for the salvation of the world. It should demonstrate the validity of the movement to restore the New Testament Church in doctrine, ordinances and life, and to promote the unity of all God's people.

This pattern of polity is not only traditional among Disciples of Christ, it is legal. It has been tested many times in the courts. *Orthodoxy and the Civil Courts* contains the oldest record of such cases. In recent times the legal basis for the freedom and independence of the local church has been upheld in such cases as Parker vs. Harper (Supreme Court of Appeals of Kentucky); Ragsdell vs. Schuler (Supreme Court of Iowa); Wright vs. Smith (Court of Appeals of Illinois); Franklin vs. Hahn (Supreme Court of Appeals of Kentucky); and Stansberry vs. McCarty (Supreme Court of Indiana). Every attempt of extra-congregational agencies, conventions or associations to compel recognition or support by local churches, or to gain possession of property, which has been contested by a majority of the members of a local church, has been decided judicially in favor of such majority. As stated in the Franklin vs. Hahn decision: "It is well established that the Christian Church groups are strictly congregational in government and activity. The local church congregation is the governing body of the church, and determination of a question by a majority of the members is final."[2]

Free congregational polity guarantees to all Christians minimal inter-ference with the individual church member's sacramental approach to his Lord, to his brethren and to his everyday workaday realities. The Catholic and the Reformation church polities have been fabricated by human acts and consist of "holy" structures which demand individual loyalties that often obscure the vital, spiritual God-man relationship which is so essential to the effectiveness of the true Church. Whatever hinders communion with Christ and fellowship with man, whatever robs man of security in the Word of Christ and the blessings which are the gift of God is as so much excess baggage in the Church that Jesus built. Nothing should separate us from the witness of the new creation in Christ, nor divorce us from the living realities of the true *Ecclesia*. Christ through the Holy Spirit must be dynamically present in the Church not only as an object of faith but at the same time a palpable demonstration of the fact that Christians have been with Jesus and learned of Him. Only so can all men know that we are His disciples. It is tragic that the monstrous ecclesiastical structures erected by men have hid this true Church from mankind. Structure there must be in a temporal world, but only the minimum depicted in the New Testament, so that all men might see the Body of Christ in all its glory.

Free church congregational polity encourages self-government beyond that of any other system. Other polities encourage the doctrine that men are incapable of self-government and discourage all attempts to exercise this inalienable and all-important right. Congregational polity provides the medium through which every Christian can exercise his birthright. It teaches him that Christ has committed churchly interests to the hands of His people, with, of course, all proper rules for their guidance. If Christ's followers are not competent to manage temporal affairs which pertain to their eternal interests in this life, how will they ever become competent to sit in judgment of the whole world at the end of time and the Last Judgment (I Corinthians 6:2).

Free church congregational polity motivates the growth of individual Christians and promotes competence in the Lord's work. Every disciple of Christ is expected to take part in the business of the Church. He recognizes his accountability to Christ for the manner in which he dis-charges tasks assigned to him. Acting under this conviction, he is constrained to seek that preparation of heart and mind which will fit him to act well his part. While it is true that not every member of the congregation takes opportunity to serve in this way, the door is open to all those who can qualify for leadership or for service in many forms. It is, however, truly amazing how many rise from insignificance to high attainments, first in the local church and then in the ministry, the mission field, evangelism, education, benevolence and social welfare. In the school of free congregationalism they learn by doing until God calls them into fields of greater usefulness.

Free church congregational polity is the most effective barrier to the development of heresy, false doctrine and general corruption. If churches are kept pure by a faithful, intelligent, God-fearing leadership that does not shun to exercise discipline when needed, there is little danger of the infiltration of apostasy. Heresy too often originates in the top echelons of extra-congregational agencies and where there is control over local churches these infidelities are transmitted into, protected and promoted within them. Where congregations have been taught to honor Christ and obey the truth as it is revealed in the Word of God, there is usually a sound majority able to express itself in congregational meetings. The unsoundness of a few individuals in the eldership, in the diaconate, or in the teaching ministry is speedily detected and eliminated when new leaders are elected. There is more danger that one man in a seat of ecclesiastical authority will become unsound and heretical than that five or one hundred will. When a pastor becomes unsound, his influence does not necessarily affect any church but his own; and this church is free to exercise its power to discipline the offender without external interference.

There is no heresy more deadly and no disloyalty more treasonable than that which for any cause or pretense whatsoever breaks up the unity of the Body of Christ, smothers the spirit of sweet communion of the saints, and the holy fellowship we have with Christ. Yet, after 150 years of general acceptance of the congregational form of government and of mutual recognition of the autonomy of the local church, there are those who would "restructure" the Church into something other than that which we now enjoy, and rob us of this freedom which our fathers purchased at great cost.

This development will receive more complete consideration in Chapter XI, but it is particularly timely and appropriate that something be said about it here.

Advocates of Restructure are saying that a new general extra-congregational church organization is essential if Disciples are to fully realize the "wholeness of the church." Because of the widespread negative reaction to this proposal, these leaders hasten to assure the Brotherhood that the freedom and autonomy of the local church would be preserved, guaranteed and made even more meaningful under the new polity. It should be noted, however, that these assurances have no legal basis or force. They are nothing but paper promises.

It should be patent to even the most naive that if there is to be restructure, there must be a change made in the old structure. The traditional structure or polity of the fellowship known as Christian Churches (Disciples of Christ) is free congregational. If it is restructured it must be something other than free congregational. It will of necessity be modified congregational, controlled congregational, combined presbyterian-congregational or episcopalian-congregational.

Disciples learned their democratic ideas in their local churches. Each local church is to them a "complete church" — complete within itself with full authority to govern all its own affairs and to choose or dismiss all its officers and ministers. These local churches are joined together only in a synthetic fellowship or loosely knit Brotherhood. They are not part of any extra congregational "national church" or "general church" organization, nor have they ever been under the direction or control of a "national" or "general constitution" or of higher governing bodies.

Should any local church consent either by official action or silent acquiescence to become a part of a Restructured Church which claimed or exercised extra-congregational authority of any kind over local churches, it would automatically forfeit its rights to present or future free autonomy. It would become something different from what it was previously. It would become an integral and legal part of "the whole church" and would be subject to all the future decisions of the extra-congregational body whether it agreed with them or not. If, under the new order, the rights of local congregations should be adjudicated in the courts, judges would in all likelihood rule that the new "Christian Church (Disciples of Christ)" is a "general church" and that churches which had been structured into it changed their character when they accepted this new status. The courts would further hold that they are no longer free congregational-type local churches, but in fact have taken on the character of parts of the general church with which they are affiliated. These churches might not be able to see the difference; they might not feel the difference; they might not yet fully know the difference. But the change would have taken place and the difference would be recognized by courts of law. The difference lies in the very character of the local church when it affiliates with a general church or denomination. In this new status local churches would be subject to all the future actions of the general church which would erode the freedoms which they once enjoyed. The general church would have the right, with approval of its highest legislative body, to repudiate all the promises that had been made to preserve and perpetuate free congregational government, and to substitute a totally different type of government.

This is no mere figment of the imagination. It should be remembered that the International Convention of Christian Churches (Disciples of Christ) is on record as favoring union with the Episcopalians, Methodists, Presbyterians, the United Church of Christ and other denominations in a plan which would almost certainly include administration by "bishops" and ordination by "episcopal" authority. If the Restructured Church does not at first compel an abandonment of the fundamental concept of free congregational polity, in which a local body of believers is affirmed to be a "complete church," then the inevitable commitments of the future will do so. Those local churches which have been caught in the web of Restructure will be forced without legal recourse to eventually surrender the last vestiges of congregational freedom in an Ecumenical World Church. But more of this anon.

Chapter VIII

MINISTERIAL FREEDOM

ON the Appalachian frontier among the free churches of Christ there was no "clergy" nor "laity."

Alexander Campbell, in his *Christian Baptist,* opposed clericalism[1] as it existed in Episcopalianism, Presbyterianism, Methodism, and to a large degree in other ecclesiastical systems. He contended that an order of bishops or elders claiming status and authority above that of the presbyters of the local church had its origin in the pagan religions and was appropriated originally by Catholicism for ulterior purposes. It partook, he believed, of the characteristics of priesthood and encouraged the injection of a certain superior and exclusive ecclesiastical pride into the simple fellowship of true Christians. Campbell was careful never to include in his criticisms "the elders of a Christian assembly, or those in the New Testament called overseers and servants of the Christian Church." In later years the sage of Bethany somewhat modified his views on the ministry, but he never admitted the validity of a superior clerical order in the Apostolic Church.

Something of the enormous influence of Campbell was indicated in the refusal of the churches on the frontier to accord the minister or pastor any status superior to the general eldership. He was considered to be an elder rendering certain special services essential to the well being of the congregation. He was often dubbed "Elder" to avoid use of the title "Reverend" which was anathema. In the community he was

79

usually known as "Elder Smith" or "Elder Jones." He was sometimes thought of as a sort of "necessary evil" guaranteeing the permanency and continuity of the local church, the maintenance of stated worship, and the discharge of "regular" duties (funerals, marriages, baptisms, etc.) which other elders could not always perform promptly because of their daily employment. He usually was "a learned man, and mighty in the Scriptures," "able both to exhort in sound teaching and to convict the gainsayers" by a clear and faithful presentation of the truth, and capable of building up the disciples in "the most holy faith" and converting others to Christ, the Way, the Truth and the Life. As an elder, the minister had the same authority in the congregation as his brother elders, such authority being expressed by the words "ruling," "government," "oversight," "watch-care," "admonition," "discipline," but as in all other matters involved in his ministry, he superintended or directed such affairs, subject to the best consensus of the entire eldership. He saw that this work was done judiciously, faithfully, impartially, and according to the law of Christ. But to compensate for such limitations, the ministers of the free churches of Christ were not subject to superintendents or bishops, church councils, or denominational disciplines. They were not bound by the social or cultural conventions imposed by the community upon the denominational clergy. They mixed with the masses, as one among them, "in the market place." They participated in their debates concerning "everything under the sun." They ministered to the needs of all their friends and neighbors whether members of their flock or not. They enjoyed a freedom which other "gentlemen of the cloth" never knew and used it well for the advancement of the kingdom of Christ.

The matter of ordination did not disturb the brethren until it became necessary to protect the churches against unworthy men, "wolves in sheep's clothing." They were not worried about "apostolic succession." There was no such thing as far as Disciples were concerned. They knew from the Scriptures that the Apostles were of a divine order with a special mission and that they could not and did not perpetuate their kind. They knew, however, about Scriptural ordination or "the laying on of hands" for the purpose of setting men apart for special ministries. So there grew up the local-church practice of examining men for ministerial qualifications and if satisfied concerning their worthiness, ordaining them and granting them licenses to preach. Sometimes these men were members of the local congregation. Sometimes they were "called men" who came to the church for approval and endowment. As important as was ordination, there was an accompanying practice of "warning the brotherhood" against unfaithful men, by the issuance of "letters to the churches." Eventually the following came to be the view of the churches regarding the pastoral ministry:

Ministers are the gift of the Lord Jesus Christ to His Church (Ephesians 4:11,12). This implies that Christ calls men to these services. The New Testament is filled with abundant evidence that He does.

Ever since the day that John the Baptist "came preaching," the Church has been indebted to God's ministers who have called sinners to repentance, preached the gospel, fed and cared for the flock of God, and instructed them in the Word of God. As long as these tasks are to be done, God will provide men to do them. Under normal circumstances local churches true to the New Testament pattern are used of God to prepare and ordain men for the ministry. But should congregations be derelict in their duty or depart from the faith, the ministry will not disappear. God will raise up men from "the valley of dry bones" to declare His Gospel to the end of the Gospel age. When a man is convinced that "necessity is laid" on him and that "woe is unto" him if he "preach not the gospel," he cannot do otherwise than become a minister. All the church councils, elders, college professors, secretaries and bishops in the world cannot prevent him. If he is truly called he will, of course, seek the counsel of faithful men of God; he will prepare himself in all that is essential to his work and will desire the ordination of an assembly of the saints. He will consider himself bound by sacred obligations to Christ and the Church and will ever seek their honor — not his own. He will preach no other gospel than that which has been delivered him in the Word of God. "He will be urgent in season and out of season; reprove, rebuke, exhort with all longsuffering and teaching . . . be sober in all things, suffer hardships . . ." and in every way "fulfill his ministry." The freedom of the minister and the freedom of the congregation are recognized as impinging somewhat the one upon the other and they may sometimes result in confusion or friction if the will and spirit of

Christ are not sought, but these freedoms cannot be denied by any human ecclesiastical power. The Christian minister is a free man in Christ!

The free man in Christ is a minister rather than a professional clergyman. Amos R. Wells has beautifully described the ministering minister:[2] "Not to sit on a lifted throne, not to rule superbly alone; not to be ranked on the left or the right in the kingdom's glory or the kingdom's might; not to be great and first of all, not to hold others in humble thrall; not to lord it over the world, a scepter high and a flag unfurled; not with authority, not with pride, vain dominion, mastery wide—nothing to wish for, nothing to do—not, in short, to be ministered to. Ah, but to minister! Lowly to sup with the servant's bread and the servant's cup; down where the waters of sorrow flow, full-baptized in the stream of woe; out where the people of sorrow are, walking brotherly, walking far; known to bitterness, known to sin, to the poor and the wretched comrade and kin; so to be helper, the last and the least, serf in the kingdom, slave at the feast, so to obey, and so to defer, and so, my Saviour, to minister. Yes, for never am I alone: this is Thy glory and this is Thy throne. Infinite Servant, well may I be bondsman and vassal and toiler — *with Thee!*"

The free man in Christ can take the Bible as his guide without being forced to accept the premises of this or that school of thought which happens to be currently approved by an ecclesiastical hierarchy. He can steep himself in the Bible, learning more and more every day what it contains and the meaning of what it contains. In patient searching under the guidance of its Author, the Holy Spirit, and in deep wrestlings of his own soul, he can come to know Christ better, he can find the treasures it contains, and he can discover the will of God for himself and his people. Thus he will learn to distinguish between the Word of God and those words of men which claim to bear witness to the Word of God. Thus the minister will become so completely dominated by the Word of God that in the striking metaphor of Jeremiah, it becomes, as it were, a burning fire shut up in his bones, by reason of which he cannot forbear to declare the Truth. He needs bear no brand but the brand of God.

It may be remembered that Alexander Campbell, who exercised this freedom with amazing zeal, once said, "I call no man master upon earth. Although my father has been a diligent student, and a teacher of the Christian religion since his youth; and, in my opinion, understands the Book as well as any person with whom I am acquainted, yet there is no man with whom I have debated more, and reasoned more, on all subjects, than he. I have been so long disciplined in the school of free inquiry, that, if I know my own mind, there is not a man upon the earth whose authority can influence me any farther than he come with the authority of evidence, reason, and truth. I have endeavored to read the Scriptures as though no one had read them before me; and I am as much on my guard against reading them (the scholars) today as I am against being influenced by any foreign name, authority or system whatever." Possibly if today we had more men of the stamp of Campbell engaged in free scholarly study of the Word of God, we would be making a greater contribution to general Biblical knowledge and understanding and to advanced ecumenical thought.

The free man in Christ need pay no tribute to any ecclesiastical device of man, such as an episcopate, a supervisory ministry, a convention, a council or an assembly. The man for whom his faith relation to Jesus Christ as the supreme disclosure of God is the one great fact that profoundly matters is a free man with respect to all else in his ministry. With the advice and consent of his brethren in the Church, he can create his own forms, devise his own instrumentalities, establish his own procedures. What he and the Church have devised they can modify, change, abandon, or replace without consulting some outer congregational authority.

The free man in Christ can express his own individuality and exercise his God-given endowments without let or hindrance. Among Disciples of Christ this freedom has produced such eminent leaders of thought and action as P. H. Welshimer, George Hamilton Combs, Charles S. Medbury, W. R. Walker, F. D. Power, Burris Jenkins, Peter Ainslee, Z. T. Sweeney, L. B. Hardeman, B. C. Goodpasture, G. C. Brewer, Ira M. Boswell, George P. Taubman, Raphael Harwood Miller, Edgar DeWitt Jones, L. N. D. Wells, B. A. Abbott, J. H. O. Smith and L. O. Bricker. These men had no pattern but Christ. Although they chose to advocate widely different views, they all built great local churches and gloried in the freedom vouchsafed to them by a Movement that had no bishops to deny them their testimony. These men and hundreds like them who gave themselves to the pastoral ministry in free churches are the finest possible evidence of the fact that it would be tragic to impose any sort of ecclesiastical "straight-jacket" on our ministry today.

The free man in Christ can speak what he believes to be the truth of God whenever and wherever he feels he is divinely compelled to do so. He is God's ambassador. God's message must be declared whether some ecclesiastical superior approves or not. Too many men act like mice in the pulpit. They mouth precise, cultured, popularly acceptable homilies. They play for headlines, tears and laughs, approval and adulation. We need men who will preach the Gospel uncompromisingly with power, speaking as before God and to dying men. Free men in Christ will naturally have such a message and will be used mightily to save the lost, renew the apathetic, and inspire the righteous to new endeavor. The late Oxford don, C. S. Lewis of *Screwtape* fame, once heard a minister close a sermon with the statement, "My dear friends, if you do not accept this truth, there may be grave eschatological consequences." "I asked him," said Dr. Lewis, "if he meant his hearers would be in danger of going to hell if they didn't believe. And when he said, 'Yes,' I replied, 'Then, why didn't you say so?'"

Perhaps, however, a word of caution needs to be spoken at this point. Liberty of opinion may be used by intemperate men to disturb the peace of the brethren, especially when merely human formulations of divine truth are made tests of fellowship. Christian ministers have no right, notwithstanding their unquestioned allegiance to Jesus Christ, to promulgate human opinions that can destroy the peace and harmony of the Church of God. Thomas Campbell, speaking on this subject said: "(I do not advocate) the renunciation of an opinion or practice . . . but merely a cessation from the publishing or practicing of it so as to give offense." Again he said: "We can neither take offense at our brother for his private opinions, if he be content to hold them as such, nor yet offend him with ours." His son Alexander Campbell frequently expressed himself in the same vein, believing that the "veering uncertainty and clashing of human opinions" is the source of most of the unhappy divisions that plague the Church.

In Volume I of the *Millennial Harbinger* is recorded the narrative of the celebrated case of Aylett Raines.[3]   Raines, a recent convert to the Restoration Movement, held views sympathetic to Universalism.   Because of them some of the brethren thought he ought to be "read out of the church."   Mr. Campbell called their attention to the clear distinction between faith and opinion.   He said, "Faith is public property; opinions are, and always have been, private property."   He did not ask Raines to give up his opinions but pled with him to keep them to himself.   Raines agreed.   Thus a threatened controversy was avoided and the peace of the brotherhood was maintained.   In later years Raines repudiated his Universalist views.

W. N. Briney has said:[4] "The Restoration movement stands for the undisputed supremacy and Lordship of Jesus Christ, and, as being necessarily involved in this, devotion to the Word that reveals Him and to the Gospel by which He must ever be proclaimed.   It stands opposed to any disposition to call in question the integrity and authority of that Word, and to the promulgation among Disciples of merely human opinions and inferences which can endanger strife.   Loyalty, liberty and fraternity are among its greatest words."

Again, the free man in Christ can face a needy world and prophetically prescribe the Biblical antidotes for its ills.   Like Habakkuk of old, he can look upon corruption and social injustice, take it as his burden and think and act as God leads him.   If courageous ministers had not seen the Lord's burden for humanity and shouldered it, we would still have slavery and child labor, there would be no progress in race relations.   Our country with its vice and violence, its God-forgetfulness, its moral callousness and selfish materialism, its racial prejudice and internal strife is full of needs and burdens which only the Gospel of Jesus Christ in its fulness and complete relevance can meet effectively.   We have a surfeit of resolutions passed in church conventions, many of them based on principles other than those to be found in God's Word.   They are adopted and forgotten.   What we need is bold challenge and courageous leadership by free ministers of righteousness so that the churches at the "grass roots" of society will become involved in Christian ways to solve local problems.   If all local churches would thus move simultaneously in consecrated Christian action, the nation's problems would be solved.

Today, ministerial freedom among Disciples of Christ is gravely threatened by a new (?) ecclesiology. It is to be found among a group of ministers who have the idea that they are superior to their brethren. They are no longer among the brethren "as those who serve" — they assume to plan, to restructure, to order, to direct. It matters little what they call themselves — presidents, secretaries, ministers of ministers, scholars, editors, professors or bishops — they are all imbued with the same spirit of overlordship. They are disposed to go beyond the New Testament pattern and to quote Scripture only to confirm their cleverly devised human schemes. They would set up orders of the ministry with ministers of local churches in the lowest category and concentrate authority in an ecclesiastical super ministry.

There is really nothing new about this development. This is exactly what happened in the third century when ambitious men moved to create a new structure for the Apostolic Church. Christ was aware of this same "mind-set" of certain religious leaders in His day. They thought themselves "qualified" to assume supreme leadership over "the flock of God." When the Master saw them in Jerusalem He said: "They make broad their phylacteries, and enlarge the borders of their garments, desire to walk in long robes, love the chief places at feasts and the chief seats in the synagogues, and love the salutations in the market-places, and to be called Rabbi." He then proceeded to give some good advice to all concerned: "Be ye not called Rabbi: for one is your teacher, and all ye are brethren. And call no man your father on earth: for one is your Father, even he who is in heaven. Neither be ye called masters: for one is your master, even Christ. But he that is greatest among you shall be your servant. And whosoever shall exalt himself shall be humbled; and whosoever shall humble himself shall be exalted."

In marked contrast to this concept of the ministry is the doctrine of Apostolic Succession which is about to be accepted in modified form by the proponents of Restructure in the Christian Churches (Disciples of Christ). It may be well at this point, therefore, to consider this doctrine. Apostolic Succession was the creation of the Catholic Bishops of the second and third Centuries for the purpose of establishing an accepted central ecclesiastical authority and controlling the leadership of the local churches. Originators of the device claimed exclusive unbroken ordained succession from the original Twelve Apostles; a claim which has never been successfully validated. These bishops set up classifications of church leadership in the following order: (1) bishops, (2) ministers or priests, (3) deacons, (4) sub-deacons, (5) lay readers, and (6) deaconesses. The last two were not to partake of the nature of Holy Orders. The bishops set up certain standards of qualification for Holy Orders, such as (1) moral character, (2) orthodoxy of belief, (3) completion of prescribed courses of instruction, and (4) conformity to Church authority. All ordinands were compelled to take a vow to obey their bishops and *facere quod facit Ecclesia* (do what the Church does).

According to the doctrine of Apostolic Succession a sharp distinction was drawn between the clergy and the laity, the former being accorded certain special privileges, exclusive rights to wear distinctive dress and insignia, and to perform charismatic rituals, rites and ceremonies. Only bishops and ministers were permitted to administer the sacraments and to preside at worship services and stated meetings of the church. The only person possessing the right to ordain to Holy Offices was the bishop. Bishops could be ordained only by a consortium of three or more bishops.

All Roman Catholic, Greek Orthodox and Anglican churches hold the doctrine of Apostolic Succession. Episcopal, Methodist, Presbyterian and Lutheran churches accept modified forms of it. This is why these ecclesiastical bodies are insisting that some form of Apostolic Succession must be adopted by the Christian Churches (Disciples of Christ) if they are to merge with the denominations represented in the current Consultation on Church Union. In the Study Document entitled *Ministry in the Christian Church (Disciples of Christ)*,[5] a humanly devised theology is set forth which would justify the following changes in our 150-year-old concepts and practices regarding the Christian ministry:

(1) The creation of a corporate ecclesiastical body which will assume control of "the whole church." It is held that only in such a visible body can the "wholeness of the church" consist.

(2) The creation of pastoral oversight over all pastors and churches through "executive ministers" or "pastors of pastors."

(3) The creation of new forms of church life and service which must be accepted by all local churches.

(4) This central organization would set up and impose conditions and limitations governing the relations of local churches with their ministers.

(5) Direct action of the local churches in the ordination of ministers would be prohibited. Examining committees of Super-Church agencies would determine by their own standards whether a man is worthy and well qualified to receive ordination. He would have to possess diplomas from approved colleges and seminaries or give assurances that he will accept and promote the official program of the Super-Church to the exclusion of all other programs. Local churches would be allowed to host the ordination services, but the duly authorized extra-congregational official representing "the whole church" would ordain.

(6) Orders of the ministry would be created: (a) licentiates, (b) ordained men and women, (c) ministers of various sorts serving local churches, (d) district counsellors and advisory ministers, (e) supervisory pastors, (f) area pastors or bishops, (g) ministers of recognized national institutions or national agencies, (h) the supreme minister of all ministers. The duties and responsibilities of the personnel in each order of the ministry would be determined by a superior ecclesiastical authority. High standards of professional excellence would be required.

(7) Control of appointments of pastors, chaplains, directors of Christian education, missionaries, teachers in schools, colleges and seminaries, administrators, general ministers, state, area and district ministers would be maintained by central headquarters.

(8) Review, evaluation and certification of ministerial standing would be made as the central offices might require.

(9) Records would be maintained to indicate to headquarters the degree of ministerial loyalty displayed in support of the official denominational program and its promotional implementation.

(10) Ministers would be required to demonstrate a high degree of

reverence for the ministerial profession and maintain reputable professional standards in all their relationships.

Only if the well-informed and alert free ministers and free churches aggressively assert their inherent Scriptural and traditional rights and privileges, and refuse to accept this proposed yoke of ecclesiastical bondage can they expect to continue completely free in Christ.

Chapter IX

FREEDOM OF ASSOCIATION

A S pointed out in previous chapters the free churches of Christ on the frontier were distinctly and irrevocably congregational in polity, but they also had a deep sense of the wholeness of the Church.[1] They were fully aware of the fact that Christ founded only one Church and that the church *at* or *in* a particular place was not the whole Body of Christ. They also knew that the Scriptural concept of the universal fellowship could never be realized in any extra-congregational human organization. They were certain that if they were to set up one themselves it could never hope to embrace all those who were members of the true Body of Christ. For this and other reasons, they refused to accept the status of a denomination. They called themselves a "Brotherhood" and sought various types of association with all those who loved the Lord and demonstrated in their daily lives a loyal, vital Christian faith.

"Brotherhood" has always been a highly significant word in the vocabulary of Disciples of Christ. They like it because it is Scriptural. The Apostle Peter calls the Church a Brotherhood. He takes for granted that all members of the Body of Christ are brothers. "Be ye all likeminded, compassionate, loving as brothers, tender-hearted, humbleminded" (I Peter 3:8). His advice to all Christians is "Above all things be fervent in your love among yourselves. Honor all men. *Love the brotherhood*" (I Peter 2:17). John, the Apostle, held the same concept. He is always saying something in his writings about Brotherhood. "He that loveth his brother abideth in the light . . ." (I John 2:10). "We know that we have passed out of death into life, because we love the brethren" (I John 3:14). ". . . we ought to lay down our lives for the brethren" (I John 3:16). To Paul the Apostle the Church is a Brotherhood. "Concerning love of the brethren," he writes to Thessalonica, "ye have no need that one write unto you, for ye yourselves are taught of God to love one another. And for indeed ye do it toward all the brethren which are in all Macedonia: but we exhort you, brethren, that ye abound more and more" (I Thessalonians 4:9,10). This is his exhortation to all Christians and he gives expression to it again and again, "In love of the brethren be tenderly affectioned one to another; in honor preferring one another" (Romans 12:10). Unless a church is a brotherhood, a company of believers whose sympathies and purposes are intertwined and whose lives are interlaced and blended, we may call it a Christian Church, but it does not bear in its body the marks of the Lord Jesus.

The Apostles got their idea of brotherhood from Jesus Christ. He constantly reminded them that He is their Master and all they are brethren. The most beautiful object lesson on brotherhood in all the Scripture is the story of how in an Upper Room He washed the disciples' feet. He cared for the dust on their feet. He was pained by the estrangement of their hearts. Finally, He gave them a commandment that was to take precedence over all His instructions which He had hitherto given them. "A new commandment I give unto you, That ye love one another. By this shall all men know that ye are my disciples, if ye have love one to another" (John 13:34, 35). And then He instituted the Lord's Supper.

The Restoration Movement has made much of the every-Sunday observance of the communion service. One of the ties that binds the churches together is the knowledge that wherever the brethren go they can gather around the Lord's Table in the Lord's House on the Lord's Day and remember His death and suffering. Here in the church's most sacred ceremony they are reminded that believers belong to one another and that the Church is a communion of brethren. In single and gathered assemblies North, South, East and West the churches are bound together in this sacred spiritual tie. Thus is the Lord's prayer in John 17 repeatedly answered. There is no fellowship more real and meaningful than this association of kindred spirits who find its complete fulfillment in Christ. No human agency, no denominational structure, no convention, no council of churches can take the place of it or be the means of realizing it more fully.

Hayden, in his *Church Polity*, clearly set forth the thinking of the best minds of this early day when he said:[2] "The kingdom of Christ, sometimes called His church, is one great community, composed of all particular communities and individual persons that have acknowledged and received Jesus of Nazareth as the Son and Messiah of God, as the only Head, King, Lawgiver and Arbiter of angels and men.

"All the particular congregations that compose this great congregation, this general assembly, called the kingdom of God, the holy nation, are responsible to one another and to the Lord as much as the individual members of any one of them are to one another and to the Lord.

"Congregations are under certain obligations to one another, the faithful discharge of which is indispensable to that free and cordial communion and co-operation essential to the holiness of the church and the triumph of the Gospel in the world.

"Among these obligations and duties are the maintenance of the doctrine and discipline of Christ's kingdom, and a due regard for all the acts and decisions of one another."

Robert Milligan, whose *Scheme of Redemption* was widely accepted as a guide in all practical concerns of the churches, said:[3] "In all purely local matters, such as pertain to their own order and discipline, the local congregations are independent of each other; and should ordinarily be allowed to manage their own affairs, according to the word of God, in whatever way they think best.

"But in all matters of general interest, such as pertain to the increase, order and power, glory and efficiency of the whole body these several congregations may and should co-operate, whenever by so doing they can better accomplish any of the great and benevolent objects for which the church was established on earth."

Alexander Campbell, a year after his election to the presidency of the

American Christian Missionary Society, wrote in the *Millennial Harbinger* (1850):[4] "Every New Testament church was absolutely independent of every other church, as much so as the different families of a community, and this must continue as our practice if we would reproduce the church of that day. If one chooses to work through a missionary society, let him do it; if one chooses to work through his own congregation, or as an individual, he must not be molested. Our societies are to stand or fall, not by the official authority of a convention, but by merit. We should not disparage the work of either, but encourage both, as long as they result in the salvation of men."

Isaac Errett, ardent supporter of many extra-congregational agencies, said[5] in an editorial in the *Christian Standard* (1867): "We have no idolatrous attachment for the General Missionary Society. If it can do the work proposed, we will encourage it. If it fails to command sufficient confidence and sympathy to enable it to do its work wisely and well, we shall go in for whatever form of associated effort the general wisdom of the brotherhood may approve."

As late as 1953, Stephen J. Corey, a former president of the United Christian Missionary Society, writing from a totally different point of view, said:[6] "We believe that since the New Testament does not provide a completed, hard and fast structural organization, in all of its details . . . the church is consequently left free to adapt forms of organization and co-operation necessary for the realistic needs and conditions of these times. This belief thus resulted in recognized missionary societies and conventions with the set-up and advisory organization needed to provide direction, consultation, inspiration, auditing and review of the work done co-operatively."

Extra-congregational co-operation was early encouraged in societies organized for the publication and dissemination of the Holy Scriptures, the planting and care of new churches, education, benevolence and many other worthy enterprises. Schools and colleges elicited the support of both individual Christians and the free churches. Without them there would have been no properly educated ministry and general education would have been without an effective Christian testimony. Such co-operation became inimical to the best interests of the churches only when authority was assumed over the churches, or when agencies adopted policies and practices not in harmony with the teachings of the Word of God. Though the unity of the church was considered to be in no way dependent upon such co-operation or association, and support of any specific agencies was never made obligatory, yet such association unquestionably promoted fellowship, unity, efficiency, progress and the general welfare of the Body of Christ.

In the early days of free association it was clearly understood that co-operation or non-co-operation was a matter of opinion and was under no circumstances to be made a test of fellowship. Thus churches and ministers of all persuasions lived together in peace and goodwill and considered one another to be members of the One Body. In many instances the constitutions and plans of work of the free associations or agencies made it clear that they (1) were expediencies, (2) were purely voluntary in character, (3) were without churchly or sacred prerogatives, and (4) were not to claim or to exercise any influence or authority over the local churches.

Today, full freedom of association or non-association is being boldly opposed by certain elements among the Disciples. Loyal support of "officially approved" associations and agencies is made a test of fellowship of equal importance to acceptance of Jesus Christ as Lord and Saviour. These extra-congregational bodies are, with approved local churches, considered to comprise the "wholeness of the Church." Such associations and agencies are being accorded churchly status and their personnel are claiming supervisory ecclesiastical authority. According to this school of thought, the brethren are not free to create new associations or agencies without the approval of some central authority. This strange new doctrine will be considered further in succeeding chapters.

Returning to M. S. Hayden, and his *Church Polity,* we find sage advice on this fourth freedom of the Free Church. In the basic aspects of his position there can be wide agreement, but some of the ideas in his work which may have been valid in his day can have dangerous implications for our times. Being human he was unable to foresee the advent of certain theological and ecclesiastical influences which were to change the climate in which freedom of association would have to be considered. However, Hayden's strong stand for Biblical Free Church polity is assurance that, if this great man were alive today, he would be on the side of full Christian freedom and fighting to preserve and promote it. Let us hear some of his finer thoughts:

"The church is a glorious fellowship. It is the perfected fruit of divine philanthropy. It is world-wide in its offers of peace and pardon, and invites to its privileges, sacrifices and honors whosoever will of every family, tribe and nation. It is not primarily an organization, but an *Ecclesia* — the called out from the world of men and women who have entered into personal and peaceful relationship with the enthroned Lord, through faith in Him and obedience to His authority. Jesus, the Christ of God, is the rock of salvation to all who are thus built upon this foundation. He is the acknowledged Head of the Church, which is called the Body of Christ. There is one head for the body and one body for the head. No body has two heads, and no head has two bodies, unless they be monstrosities . . .[7]

"It is absolutely certain that Jesus founded one church, and only one church, on earth. There can be but one 'holy, catholic church' within the territory of this world. Hence the unity of the church is generally assumed, but sometimes declared, in the apostolic writings. Sects may be numerous, as they are, but it is an awful crime to rend the body of Christ . . .[8]

"The Scriptural conception of the unity of the Christian church is not realized in any ecclesiastical organization . . . It is equally certain that the one church of Jesus Christ is visibly represented in this world in the local congregations of His disciples, covenanted together for Christian fellowship, service and worship . . . Separate assemblies, necessitated by mere convenience, for the performance of public duties and the enjoyment of religious privileges are not different bodies, possessing all the powers and performing all the functions of a complete and independent organism. They are severally members of the general body, each doing its own work in harmony with its vital connection with the larger organization of which it is a part . . .[9]

"These local churches sustain mutual relations and owe mutual obligations to each other. There is unity in these pluralities. They stand on the same doctrinal basis which is their bond of union. Paul expands the bond of peace into seven items . . . 'There is one body and one Spirit, one hope, one Lord, one faith, one baptism, one God and Father of all, who is above all and through all and in you all' (Ephesians 4:4-6). Therefore they are all under the same ecclesiastical law, the revealed will of the one Lord, and constitute the holy temple in the Lord in whom they are builded together for an habitation of God through the Spirit (Ephesians 2:21-22). This binds them to the observance of the same ordinances and to be governed by the supreme law of love to God and to each other . . . Having the same rule of discipline, they are mutually bound to respect the acts of each other so far as they accord with that rule. (Sister churches should stand ready to extend help to afflicted sister churches whether the trouble be doctrinal or disciplinary whenever such help is desired.) . . . Christian obligation is placed upon all alike, and duty enjoined upon one company of believers rests upon all companies of Christ's followers with equal weight. Otherwise all Christian obligation ceased with the primitive age. The ground principle of the sufficiency of the New Testament as a rule of faith and discipline assumes that the instruction of the Apostles to each particular church of their age binds all modern churches under like circumstances to do the same things . . .[10]

"Co-operation, local and general (is primarily) for self-edification and the world's evangelization. There is and can be no effectual working for these evangelical purposes without such co-operation . . . In co-operative unity of churches of Christ, there is strength to overcome the world and to overthrow all forms of unbelief and irreligion . . .

"The time has fully come when the spirit of love, loyalty and lowliness should so fill all the house where the redeemed hosts of God are sitting in heavenly places, that they will all speak the same thing as the Spirit gives them utterance, that there be no divisions among them, but that they all be perfectly joined together in the same mind and in the same judgment as becomes saints."[11]

Free association in the larger tasks of the universal church is a Christian imperative in a world that is increasingly dominated by pagan ideologies and movements. In unity there is strength and the unity of free churches of Christ is the most adaptable and effective unity in the world. Free churches are the only churches which, while retaining their liberty in Christ, can exert that diversity and flexibility in thought and action, so essential to meeting emerging needs in a world which is as rapidly changing as ours.

The only limit to the freedom of local churches in co-operative effort should be the love they bear to Christ and to one another as brethren in Christ. They cannot give *carte blanche* submission to extra-congregational authority, for this would destroy the free unity of believers in their common apprehension of truth, and their common effort to make the truth as they see it completely effective in their own lives and the lives of men in a worldly society. If choice has to be made between unity and freedom in action Christian churches must choose freedom, for a church lacking in freedom is not a true church. As Matthew Spinka has put it, in his *Quest for Church Unity*,[12] "God is freedom to those who love Him; He is law only to those who rebel against Him. No one can be forced to accept God's proffered grace; but once he becomes a member of Christ's body he cannot be cut off from it except by his own act." No Super Church or human organization claiming to be "the whole church" can determine bonds of fellowship, nor compel courses of action for local churches. Fellowship in a common task must be motivated by love and by a common desire to do the will of Christ, or the undertaking has no valid Christian meaning to those who participate. The principle of unity in freedom motivated and limited only by love is essential to true Christian co-operation.

Having established this fact, it is equally true that isolationism is a sin against love of Christ and the brethren. Fellowship, the communion of saints, a sense of oneness with other believers who are members of the one Body in Christ, and a desire to work with all Christians for the accomplishment of the will and purpose of Christ *must not be neglected!* Such neglect will destroy the *koinonia* which is essential to the true Church. On the other hand, he who breaks the *koinonia* by asserting superior authority, jurisdiction or theological knowledge sins against love and stands as guilty before God as those who refuse or neglect to associate with brethren in worthy tasks. Although free churches have a right to a distinct and meaningful existence relevant to the peculiar situations in which they may be found, and to an equality with one another, yet they are obligated to preserve union and communion with one another, since they are all united in Christ. This union and communion must be visible and realistic, demonstrating to each other and to the world that they bear the marks of true Christian churches and that they are seeking the same goals, accomplishing the same purposes and rendering the same services to which they have been divinely called. This mutual relationship and fellowship need not be limited to a humanly-devised pattern or organization superimposed upon the churches, but rather marked by a divine pattern of Christian brotherhood which has its strength and power in love, liberty and loyalty to Christ.

This chapter should not end without some reference to a new grassroots movement in the church life of modern America. There is a widespread revolt against the restraints imposed by the rigid co-operative programs of institutional Christianity. Without any fanfare and with little publicity a new Christian community is being born. Everywhere one sees hundreds of independent Baptist, Bible, Apostolic, Christian or Evangelical churches, tabernacles, temples or centers which have little or no relationship to organizations with any centralized authority. It is estimated that the total membership of these churches runs well into the millions. Exercising their divine right of freedom of association hundreds of groups are springing up, without benefit of central ecclesiastical authority, to bring the Christian message to college campuses, to factories and to suburban communities. Independent "cells" and "coffee houses" are being formed, under the very eyes of the traditional churches, where earnest prayer is being offered and serious discussion and independent Bible study are being pursued. Here Christian answers are being sought in unorthodox ways for individual and social problems, and efforts are being made to discover deeper spiritual and pragmatic meaning for all of life. Such a knowledgeable person as "Billy" Graham estimates[13] that there are over a million such free associations of earnest souls already in existence and that the number is growing daily. There are no class distinctions in these groups, no racial or denominational barriers. These people are literally being forced into such independent action because many of the conventional churches are so busy with paper programs issued from headquarters, with meeting denominational budget quotas, and with greasing the many wheels within wheels of ecclesiastical machinery, that they have little time for free vital personal religion. This new grassroots movement is giving a practical demonstration of the effectiveness of the Christian principle of freedom of association which is inherent in the Free Church. Will the conventional churches "get the message" of this modern "handwriting on the wall" and return both to the prime business of the Church and to its Apostolic polity? If they do not, we are probably witnessing the beginnings of a new Free Church movement in America operating outside the aegis of formal traditional Christianity. And this would not be the first time that seekers after the true faith have had to go "outside the gates" to recapture its esoteric reality.

Chapter X

CORPORATIVE CO-OPERATION

THE story of the rise of extra-congregational corporative co-operation among Disciples of Christ is long and controversial.[1] It is marked by large achievement to the glory of God, but also by bitter debate and open schism. Involved in the story are many factors — theological, ethical, social and ecclesiastical — but our concern in this study is primarily in the field of church polity.

As has been previously stated, early co-operative endeavors were considered to be (1) expediences, (2) voluntary associations, (3) without churchly or sacred prerogatives, and (4) without any right to exercise guidance or authority over local congregations. They were not believed to be in any sense "the church," nor considered essential to "the wholeness of the Church." They were simply "servants" of those churches and/or individuals who desired to avail themselves of their services.

The rise of these "agencies," as they were often called, began with the organization of the American Christian Bible Society in 1845 for the distribution of the Holy Scriptures. It co-operated with the Baptist Bible Union and the American and Foreign Bible Society and finally disbanded to work through the latter organization for the achievement of its purpose. Then came the Sunday School and Tract Society in 1848 "to diffuse the knowledge of the Christian religion, by the publication and circulation of religious tracts, and a Sunday School library, with special reference to the wants of our brotherhood, and the interests of our children."

About the year 1849 there seemed to be a general feeling that some kind of national organization should be formed which would enable all the brethren to work together in tasks which could be done better co-operatively than singly or exclusively. In a series of articles published in the *Millennial Harbinger*, in that year, entitled, "Church Organization," Alexander Campbell discussed the organization of the local church and pointed out the advantages of co-operation on a larger scale. He proposed a meeting of interested brethren, and on October 23, 1849, a group of 156 convened in Cincinnati, Ohio, to explore possibilities. Before they adjourned they organized the American Christian Missionary Society, elected Campbell president *in absentia,* and prepared to encourage a co-operative program of evangelism at home and abroad. By 1868, however, its accomplishments had been so meager that the brethren appointed a committee to provide a better means of co-operation.

The following year the notorious "Louisville Plan"[2] was launched. It called for a general convention composed of messengers from state conventions, who would be chosen by representatives of the churches and district conventions, the latter being composed of messengers from the churches. There were to be general, state and district boards corresponding to the various conventions, and each constituent body was to have a corresponding secretary and an executive officer. Each state was entitled to two delegates, plus one additional for each five thousand members in the state. Churches were to pledge definite sums annually for missions and pay it to the district treasurer who was to divide it into two equal sums for the district and the general boards. How men of supposedly good judgment, committed to the principle of congregational freedom could have been persuaded that this was the solution to the problems of the brotherhood continues to be a marvel. When the news of the "Plan" was read by the churches they were literally astounded. The brethren could not understand why they should have such an elaborate ecclesiastical system foisted upon them so soon after their liberation from denominationalism. Financial support was withdrawn.

The machinery failed to operate. The cause of extra-congregational co-operation was set back a full decade.

The utter failure of the "Louisville Plan" temporarily convinced the Disciples that complicated ecclesiastical mechanisms are not according to their genius as a religious movement; that individual and congregational freedom cannot be discounted; that missionary contributions must be voluntary and elicited by the merit of the work; that co-operation of the churches must be a purely voluntary matter and any plan of federating them into an official organization would be unacceptable to many of them; that the support of extra-congregational societies or conventions cannot be made a test of fellowship if any semblance of unity and brotherhood is to be maintained; and that sometimes things have to get worse before they get better. The death of the "Louisville Plan" did not prove that the brethren were opposed to co-operation or to missionary work, but only that new patterns would have to be devised which would accomplish these laudable ends without threatening the genius of the movement.

Various changes were made from time to time in the structure of the General Christian Missionary Convention until finally it retained but few of the objectionable features of the "Louisville Plan." Its missionary work eventually resumed the old name, American Christian Missionary Society, and it continued until its absorption in the United Christian Missionary Society in 1920. In 1874 two encouraging developments in co-operation had their inception — the Christian Woman's Board of Missions and the Foreign Christian Missionary Society. From their beginnings they had wide support. Under their auspices the churches saw missionary work spread to many lands and thousands of souls won to Christ.

In various states and regions other "missionary societies" were organized, beginning with the Ohio Christian Missionary Society[3] established at Wooster in 1852. The chief task of these bodies was the evangelization of their areas and the planting of new churches of Christ. There was a clear understanding among the churches that no super-church organization nor any exercise of quasi-official authority by state or regional evangelists would be tolerated. They rejected the delegate idea and favored mass meetings of interested brethren. Churches or ministers that doubted the wisdom of such co-operation, disapproved policies, or simply neglected the fellowship, were still considered brethren.

The rapid expansion of the Restoration Movement in all parts of the nation created the problem of financing adequate church buildings. Accordingly the Board of Church Extension was organized in 1881. Within 25 years it became a multi-million dollar "building and loan" enterprise and eventually grew into one of the wealthiest and most widely supported national agencies. As brotherhood conscience directed, there came such agencies as the National Benevolent Association (1886), the Board of Ministerial Relief (1895), the Board of Temperance (1907), the National Bible (Sunday) School Association (1908), and the Association for the Promotion of Christian Unity (1914). In somewhat the same category had come the development of numerous schools and colleges, beginning with Transylvania (1836) and Bethany (1840). Each had its own charter, was responsible for raising its own funds, was owned and operated by its independent self-perpetuating board of trustees, and enjoyed full academic freedom. From the beginning of the movement there had been a "free press" — competitive, privately owned, self-perpetuating publishing houses — which produced all kinds of literature used by the churches. There were no official publications, each church freely providing for its needs on the basis of the evident merits of the product.

On the 100th anniversary of the publication of Thomas Campbell's *Declaration and Address*, the success of this Free Church movement was amply attested in the great Centennial Convention[4] in Pittsburgh, Pennsylvania, which drew over 30 thousand people from all parts of the nation and from foreign lands. No gathering of the brethren ever equaled it before nor since. The brotherhood had grown from about 20 persons to a million and a half. It was the most rapidly growing religious communion in America. The gathering reached its climax in the reports of the marvelous accomplishments of the free agencies and in the enormous Communion Service which overflowed Forbes Field. More than 30 thousand people partook of the emblems of Christ's death and suffering on a Lord's Day afternoon while the whole nation marveled at how God had blessed this peculiar people who had no creed but Christ, no book of discipline but the New Testament, no name but the divine, and no government but heaven's.

But almost simultaneously with this triumph came the first great schism in the Restoration Movement.[5] It is impossible in this limited work to consider all the reasons why 2,649 congregations withdrew from their brethren in 1906 and set up the separate communion known as the Church of Christ. But one of the chief factors was fear of the growing influence of the agencies in the life of the free churches. There had long been a considerable element in the Brotherhood that considered the introduction of extra-congregational societies a dangerous development, "a departure from the principles for which we have always contended as sanctioning the charter of expediency, the evil and pernicious effects of which the past history of the Church fully proves." This opposition may be concisely stated in three forms: (1) the conviction that all human ecclesiastical organizations are unauthorized by the Scriptures, and are therefore unscriptural; (2) the potential danger of the societies or agencies infringing upon the independence of the local churches; and (3) the making of a particular kind of co-operative endeavor a test of Christian fellowship. Our Church of Christ brethren have demonstrated in a truly amazing fashion that extra-congregational corporate agencies are not essential to growth and prosperity. Today they number 2,300,000 members in 16,500 churches and support a tremendous complex of evangelists, missionaries, schools and colleges, benevolent homes, radio and television programs.

Following the Centennial Convention the agencies entered upon an unprecedented era of prosperity. Serving the "mainstream" of the Restoration Movement and freed from the incubus of perennial opposition from right-wing extremists, they burgeoned in material wealth, practical efficiency and statistical success. Wise leadership considered the agencies to be voluntary service associations without ecclesiastical status, and exercising no undue influence over the local churches. As Loren E. Lair has so succinctly put it[6] in his book, *The Christian Churches and Their Work*, "This was in keeping with (1) the desire for many societies within the brotherhood, (2) the individualistic approach which gave freedom to any person or church to organize and secure support for a need, (3) the fear of a too-powerful organization on a national scale, and (4) the manner in which Disciples gave support to their organizations, namely, by individual and specific appeals to interested individuals and churches." By 1917 there existed, without any national connectional relationship, 40 state missionary societies, 34 institutions providing some form of higher education, 9 national boards or societies, 2 major publishing houses, dozens of monthly periodicals and journals, and a national assembly or mass meeting which provided an open forum for anyone who wished to attend.

Then arose a generation who "knew not Joseph." Before them was spread out a more or less complete pattern of extra-congregational corporative associations which had an appearance of denominational congruity. With critical eyes they detected a certain amount of "irresponsibility," "confusion" and "competition" which might be corrected by the creation of a strong connectional but "democratic" national organization frankly "denominational" in nature. An immense "promised land" spread out before them. It could well be possessed by an "enlightened leadership." It could well attain proud status as "one of the great denominations of Christendom."

Into this situation came the Campbell Institute, an organization of several hundred sophisticated and ambitious ministers and educators who had "seen the light" theologically and ecclesiastically. Significantly, *Disciples of Christ: A History* notes[7] that "through this fellowship there flowed much of the vital substance nourishing the growing edge of the Disciples . . . A neglected theme is the achievement in practical nurture of the churches, in evangelism and other promotional work, by men of this fellowship." In 1939 the *Christian Standard* pointed out that "six of the last eight presidents of the International Convention" were members of the Institute. A list of prominent men in the work of all the colleges and agencies covering a period of 50 years from 1909 reveals the extent to which Institute men came to control "the organized life of the Brotherhood."

What was happening here was the creation of an Establishment[8] which was to take over actual behind-the-scenes control in all the extra-congregational agencies of the Disciples. In a scholarly and trenchant paper[9] read by Paul M. Harrison before the Oberlin conference (1963) of the Consultation on Church Union, this Princeton professor distin-

guished between "legal authority" and "actual power" in church government. He elaborated: "Given the disparate nature of authority and
power in the participating denominations it can be reasonably hypothe-
sized that one of the most effective instruments for . . . formulating
denominational polity is one of the most difficult to define. In secular
political literature it has been called 'The Establishment' . . . The Establishment appears to be a functional necessity in all denominations. The
first order of business of every informed Establishment meeting is to
deny the existence of the Establishment. The leaders of the Establishment maintain that real denominational power rests with the people,
the local congregations, the regional officers, the national executives,
and the general assembly . . . but —." The remainder of Dr. Harrison's
paper gives a limited description of the way the Establishment really
works. He said that there is a little coterie of professional clergymen,
business and professional men, ecclesiastical executives and theologians
of various persuasions (except "fundamentalists" and "bibliolaters")
who get together from time to time and decide what the program of
the denomination will be and what strategies will be necessary in
the so-called representative conventions. They are supported by two
or three "big men" in the public eye, some representatives of the
socially elite and a handful of affluent laymen who can undergird the
budget. This small body of "key men" can hold the balance of power
in executive and board meetings and exert the necessary influence in
the right places to insure the election or appointment of the "right
people" to all important positions in the ecclesiastical machine. The
Establishment is usually made up of "near-conservatives" and "almost
radicals" who co-operate to discover the non-irritating approaches to
controversial issues and know what "wires to pull" to get approval in
"representative" bodies for the policies and programs which are "in
the best interests of the churches." This Princeton scholar's description
aptly fits the Disciples' Establishment which first envisioned before
World War I[10] the creation of a massive inclusive centralized denominational structure and began to move in 1917-19, first, to "Unify";
then, to "Co-ordinate"; and finally, to "Restructure" the Brotherhood.[11]

The Establishment made an abortive effort in 1910 to transform
the General Christian Missionary Convention from a mass meeting

into "one general delegate Convention"; and the national agencies from independent corporations into "boards" of the Convention. Voted down overwhelmingly, this did not deter them. They effected a compromise in 1917 which permitted the brethren to meet in a mass assembly known as the International Convention of Disciples of Christ, but transferred virtual control of the vital Convention machinery to a "Committee on Recommendations."[12]

An attempt was then made to merge all the six major national agencies into the United Christian Missionary Society. The merger was effected at the Cincinnati Convention in 1919, but such a protest went up from the free churches that in the early years of the 1930-40 decade, the Board of Church Extension, the Pension Fund (formerly the Board of Ministerial Relief), and the National Benevolent Association withdrew. This left in the UCMS only the old American Christian Missionary Society, the Foreign Christian Missionary Society, and the Christian Women's Board of Missions.

Not to be blocked in its program of "Unification,"[13] the Establishment saw the UCMS as a medium through which semi-official advisory and/or supervisory authority might be effectively exercised over state and regional agencies and in functional areas which had not yet been appropriated by other corporative associations. Accordingly the UCMS set up new divisions, departments, commissions and committees in a staggeringly comprehensive ecclesiastical system involving almost every conceivable operation of a "responsible denomination." (See Chapter XI, p. 116.)

As a result of this attempt of the Establishment to forge the chains of centralized corporative co-operation upon the free churches, there was another major break in the ranks of the Brotherhood. It began at Cincinnati in 1919 and reached its climax at Memphis in 1926. Polity was not the only factor in this development, but the principles of congregational freedom and freedom in co-operative enterprise were of major concern. At this time many new so-called "free agencies" were organized to serve the churches in the fields of evangelism, missions, education, and benevolence. Their advent was accompanied by enlarged achievement in all of these areas. For example, not a single new mission station was opened by the so-called "official agencies" from 1918-1942, not a single new college was founded, and few new churches were planted. In this same period the new "free agencies" established hundreds of new churches; won multiplied thousands to Christ; set up ten new educational institutions training hundreds of ministers, missionaries and full-time Christian workers; organized many new homes for the aged and for children; established two new hospitals; and planted scores of new missions in 11 foreign lands. A new national mass meeting called the North American Christian Convention was launched a year after Memphis, which now registers nearly 20,000 brethren annually and gives promise of becoming one of the largest religious conventions in America. It is estimated that this group of so-called "independents" now number over 1,300,000 members in some five thousand churches. Many of them are still listed in the official *Yearbook of the Christian Churches* (Disciples of Christ). Theirs is a mighty testimony for the Free Church and the freedoms which its polity affords. So far these brethren have caused no public schism but such a tragic event could well come as a result of "Restructure."

Despite the merger effected at Cincinnati, "Unification" was not complete. Several national boards and agencies were not included in the new ecclesiastical structure. The national agencies were not yet completely "responsible" creatures of the national convention. The state missionary societies were separate entities. The institutions of higher education retained their independence. The Establishment, therefore, moved from a policy of "Unification" to one of "Co-ordination."

The strategy of the Establishment was now to gain control of the financial processes undergirding all of the agencies at every level of Brotherhood life and force unification. The International Convention was persuaded to establish (1923) a Commission on Budgets and Promotional Relationships. By 1934 the Convention moved to create Unified Promotion. Through these two structures all the agencies of the Brotherhood accepted a united fiscal, promotional and strategic program. They were persuaded that all overlapping and impinging programs should be eliminated, that new structures should be created, that new methods be devised to achieve complete unification and co-ordination, and, finally, that centralized administrative controls be accepted. The finesse with which the Establishment directed this operation is attested by the fact that the agencies themselves, through the Convention-created Council of Agencies, took all the necessary steps to destroy their own freedom and forge the shackles of their own servitude.

Through the Council of Agencies another very significant metamorphosis took place: It supervised and promoted the "Long Range Planning Program" of 1950-1960 and the "Decade of Decision Program" of 1960-1970, which carried the objectives of the Establishment and the central hierarchy down to the local churches at the "grassroots" level of the Brotherhood. The spiritual and ecclesiastical "window dressing" made these programs very plausible. The local churches welcomed release from the onerous task of planning their own programs. They could now follow the directions from headquarters prepared by experts in all the functional activities of the church. They were privileged to "goose step" with all the other "co-operative churches" in the achievement of "effective ministry, evangelism, stewardship, budget relationships, curriculum, church growth and development, service to racial groups, social welfare, world outreach, missionary policy, ecumenical strategy, and the best in local church life." The churches revelled in the satisfaction of being "co-operative," "united," "responsible" and "approved." Most of them, however, were unaware of the price they were being psychologically conditioned to pay. The cost was ultimate loss of congregational autonomy and freedom of action through acceptance of "Restructure."

The major purpose of the Decade of Decision program was to assure the "Restructure" of the Brotherhood. It is devoutly hoped by its advocates that the necessary educational, promotional, organizational and judicial steps can be taken in the decade 1960-1970 thus completing the corporate ecclesiastical metamorphosis which the Establishment had "dreamed about before World War I."

This program of Restructure, so crucial in the life of the Free Churches, will be treated in some depth in the next chapter.

Chapter XI

RESTRUCTURE

DESPITE the tragic defections of thousands of Free Churches in the early 1900s and 1920s, the Disciples' Establishment now decided to move beyond "Unification" and "Co-ordination" to "Restructure."

At this same time, many brethren of widely differing doctrinal persuasions were beginning to express deep concern about the divided state of the Brotherhood and to seek some means by which real internal unity might be achieved. In 1959 Wichita, Kansas, was the scene of an important Consultation on Internal Unity of Christian Churches. Here problems were discussed in good spirit with encouraging results. Then followed meetings at Wichita in 1960, Stillwater, Oklahoma, in 1961, Tulsa, Oklahoma, in 1962, Saint Louis, Missouri, in 1964, and Enid, Oklahoma, in 1966.

A few men of high standing in the International Convention viewed with deep concern the trends toward the creation of a strong centralized ecclesiastical structure. Winfred E. Garrison, one of the most widely respected scholars and leaders in the Brotherhood, spoke out boldly in an address[1] at the Kansas City Assembly (1961): "If it is true that our aim is a unity of all Christians that will not be conditioned upon universal subscription to any substantial body of doctrine or the acceptance of one all-embracing ecclesiastical structure, then it is the duty and privilege of the Disciples of Christ to give the world an object lesson of the possibility of such unity. We have an unprecedented opportunity to demonstrate to all observers that it is possible for a wide variety of doctrinal views, and also a variety of separate agencies for carrying on Christian work, to exist peacefully and fraternally within one body of Christians. I refuse to admit that those Disciples who do not co-operate with the agencies represented in this Convention do not, on that account, belong to 'us.' If they do not, it is not for that reason. These particular agencies through which we do our co-operative work are good and useful, and I would urge redoubled support of them. But they are not the basis and ground of our fellowship. I would hate to see the form of words we use in taking a convert's confession of faith developed into: 'Do you believe that Jesus is the Christ and do you agree to support the UCMS?' "

The Establishment viewed these ameliorating developments with a mixture of disdain and alarm and moved with new-born determination to achieve their long-desired ends. A Committee on Brotherhood Restructure, appointed at the Denver Assembly, reported at Louisville (1960). Its Report[2] contained an exhaustive treatment of "The Rationale of Restructure," "The Breadth and Depth of Restructure," "Ways and Means of Restructure" and "Financial Support." The Report said that all previous efforts toward reorganization were inadequate, involving only the agencies which report to the Convention. It insisted that "outmoded procedures" be abandoned and that "a new and imaginative church structure" be devised. It conceded the fact that originally the Disciples had been committed to a Free Church polity, but this was due to poor means of communication on the frontier and to a lack of intelligent leadership. Early extra-congregational organizations, said the Report, were created for purely pragmatic reasons and were given no official character. Lacking any theology of the Church beyond the local congregation, and refusing to accept denominational status, the churches considered themselves part of a vague Christian unity movement. They felt that a denominationally structured communion would hinder their broad goals. However, the unity movement failed, said the Report, and the Disciples became a separate but irresponsible denomination. It concluded that "no matter what we started out to be," the Disciples are now in deed and in fact a denomination and should act in a "responsible fashion." The Brotherhood should become more than "the sum total of local congregations" and assume the status of a *Church*.

The Louisville Report then turned to future action, proposing that the Disciples develop a new theology of the nature and mission of the Church and proceed to restructure for bigger and broader "involvement" in keeping with an "overall master plan which will relate each part to the whole." The new structure should extend beyond our own borders, including our "historic concern for Christian unity." The time has come, the Report said, to "quit tinkering with the machinery" and seek a new design "rooted in a new Christian conviction concerning the Church." It boldly stated that *every level* in the Brotherhood should be involved in a new denominational structure including "its church members, its ministry, its function, its authority, city unions, district and state conventions and organizations, its International Convention and all agencies reporting to it, colleges, seminaries, benevolent homes, national planning bodies and involvement in all ecumenical bodies." The words "autonomy" and "self-government" should be scrapped, said the Committee, and replaced by "inter-dependence" and "responsibility." The freedom of the local church should be impregnated with a new sense of obligation to proper official authority.

At Louisville it was evident that the Establishment had embarked upon a ruthless policy, determined to achieve Restructure with all due speed regardless of the costs involved. Loren E. Lair, who was president of the International Convention that year, made the statement[3] that "We must have an organization that can move together if we are to have an effective witness. This needs to be achieved, even if it means a breaking away of the anti-organization wing of the Christian Churches, a possible loss of 2,700 churches and 650,000 members." Similar expressions were heard in the night sessions of the Campbell Institute, traditional rendezvous for liberal thinking and planning, where many leaders of the Restructure movement spoke. The Louisville Assembly approved the Report of the Committee and authorized the appointment of a Commission on Brotherhood Restructure of 120 to 130 persons, and Restructure of the Brotherhood in depth and breadth.[4]

The brethren assembled at Louisville seemed unaware of the fact that Restructure was already being realized in many ways under supervision of the Establishment. A Panel of Scholars had been at work since 1956 drafting the tentative blueprint. Their findings were now published in three volumes under the general title, *The Renewal of Church:* (1) *The Reformation of Tradition,* (2) *Reconstruction of Theology,* and (3) *Revival of the Churches.* Many other volumes designed to prepare church leaders for the abandonment of the Restoration tradition, including the Free Church idea, had long been in circulation and were now promoted with new enthusiasm. Actual restructuring of state and regional "missionary societies" and "associations" was proceeding step by step as rapidly as the opposition would permit. National agencies were being persuaded to change their constitutions and by-laws so that all legal barriers to complete involvement with the new centralized ecclesiastical structure would be removed. The fact is, that more was being accomplished in Restructure behind the scenes by pressures from the Establishment than in the much publicized open "democratic" actions of the duly constituted corporative associations of the brethren.

The next most significant official development in Restructure was the adoption by the Detroit Assembly (1964) of a pronouncement[5] entitled, "The Nature of the Structure the Brotherhood Seeks." It was a carefully drafted theological and philosophical statement of the fundamental principles of Restructure. Dr. Granville T. Walker, then chairman of the Commission on Brotherhood Restructure, termed it "the basic document of the movement." It is a pious, plausible and persuasive thing with which few might take serious exception, *unless* they were capable of interpreting its true meaning and significance in the light of historic trends in the thought and life of the Brotherhood, and of a complete awareness of the structural changes being contemplated by the Establishment. Actually, this document is widely accepted as a *carte blanche* apologetic for all the structural changes to be made in the next ten years.

Section by section the document gives tacit approval of (1) a comprehensive reorganization of every phase of Brotherhood life from the local church to the national Convention; (2) revolutionary changes beyond Restructure in order to perpetually adjust the churches to new social and religious developments; (3) a new official interpretation of such traditional terms as "freedom," "authority," "responsibility," "rights," "autonomy" and "power" in light of the above changes; (4) whatever alterations may be necessary "under God" in functions, freedoms, responsibilities, systems, autonomies and limitations; (5) some later-to-be-determined guarantee of unity and diversity in matters of opinion; (6) complete involvement in the policies and programs of area, national and world Councils of Churches, and whatever ecclesiastical mergers may be necessary to achieve "One Church for One World"; and (7) new powers for national headquarters so that they may control all aspects of "Christian stewardship." Through these powers local congregations and agencies can be compelled to give their material resources only to Establishment-approved agencies and programs. The major thrust of this article is that true religion can best be advanced by means of the organization which will result from Restructure. Its framers seem obsessed by the fatal error which has plagued church officialdom for centuries—that well-heeled, efficient power structures can best advance the kingdom of God.

The Detroit Assembly also received a Progress Report[7] which said, in effect, that Restructure would honor the principle of representative government, include every "manifestation" of the Church in its organization and develop a "covenant" which would bind all the "manifestations" together.[8] The Assembly also received a detailed plan to convert the International Convention into a delegate body[9] and to change its name so as to constitute it "The Christian Church (Disciples of Christ)." More of this anon.

After Detroit, Restructure proceeded at a greatly accelerated pace. We record some of the more recent achievements:

(1) *Local Churches*. Most local churches are loath to part with their traditional congregational freedom. Without seeming to ask for endorsement of Restructure, local churches are being advised by representatives of the Establishment to adopt new constitutions and by-laws. These proposed legal documents are drawn in such a fashion as to link the church irrevocably to the denomination and thereby to whatever form of Restructure it may adopt.[10]

Some of the ways in which the freedom of the local churches is already beginning to be affected are: (a) Their freedom is spoken of as permissive, not inherent or of divine right. (b) They are being denied the right of ordaining ministers without extra-congregational approval. (c) Churches are being required to call and dismiss ministers only upon headquarters advice. (d) They are being pressured to accept only programs of work, service and witness drafted by a central planning agency. (e) Their fiscal affairs must be conducted according to a general pattern of "Christian Stewardship" drafted by headquarters. (f) Support of extra-congregational agencies and co-operation in interdenominational must be approved by general executive pastors or bishops.

This list of threats to congregational autonomy could be extended, but these citations should be sufficient to convince Disciples of Christ that the "freedom" being promised the local churches by advocates of Restructure is nothing more than a mirage in a desert of centralized ecclesiastical power. (Read again Chapter VII, pages 71-76.)

(2) *The Ministry.* We have already discussed the changes made and proposed with respect to the Christian ministry. (Read again Chapter VIII, pages 86-89.)

(3) *States or Areas.* For several years Restructure has been going on at state and regional levels. New constitutions and by-laws have been adopted which (a) strengthen the ties of the organization with national denominational headquarters, (b) set up controlled delegate conventions, (c) provide "pastoral oversight" of congregations and ministers, (d) set up official promotional programs of service and work which follow the master pattern devised by national headquarters. In some areas the old "state societies" have been reconstructed into "area churches" and "state secretaries" have assumed the title of "area ministers" or "area bishops." Southern California furnishes the finest example of this development.[12]

In 1962 the state organization of Southern California set up a Committee on a Strategy for the Christian Church in Southern California which produced a comprehensive report involving every phase of its structure and life. In 1965 the final official action of a delegate convention created an Area Church, as "the co-operative expression of the various congregations (local churches) of Christian Churches

(Disciples of Christ) in Southern California and Nevada." This Area Church has an Area Assembly which is designated as the official legislative body "composing the church in action" while in session. This Area Church determines the agencies which local churches may support and also the agencies which they are not permitted to support. It determines the programs of work which shall be carried on by local churches. The Area Church is given full and final authority in the ordination of ministers of local churches and must approve the calling and releasing of ministers by local churches. The Area Church has a general executive minister or bishop who has oversight of all the churches and supervision of every phase of the churches' work and witness in the Area. There are also on the headquarters staff "associate ministers" and "program specialists" who have extra-congregational authorities and, together with the Area bishop, determine whether the national programs of work and witness are faithfully implemented. The Area Church is also given full and final authority in effecting mergers with other denominations and determining what forms of interdenominational co-operation are satisfactory.

All Area Churches and other-type regional organizations[13] have been warned that, as Restructure nears fulfillment, the number and boundaries of such entities may be subject to further changes. These changes will come from properly designated national authorities and will be "determined by theological considerations, geography, economic base, political divisions, number of members, number of congregations, centers of communication, transportation facilities, financial strength, educational facilities, population shifts, and relationship to program flow and services." Word has come down from Restructure leaders that since new responsibilities for pastoral oversight and control of the churches will be required of the Area bishops, regional structures smaller than the now-existing state/area organizations may lend themselves to a more efficient ecclesiastical operation.

(4) *National Agencies.* The best example of Restructure at the national level is the United Christian Missionary Society. Since the merger of seven major national agencies was authorized in Cincinnati in 1919, the UCMS has become far more than a missionary organization. As pointed out in Chapter X, it goes as far as is humanly

possible in lieu of legal authority in supervising the "work of the Brotherhood." It has committees and societies in all state and regional organizations, and in as many local churches as permit them. It has complete machinery in its Department of Religious Education for serving the Sunday Schools and controlling curriculum. This Department maintains a liaison relationship with the Christian Board of Publication. Departments of Resources, Service, Missionary Education, Social Welfare, etc., involve almost every conceivable operation of a "responsible" denomination. Committees and commissions deal with town and country problems, urban work, church development, ministerial services, military and veterans' services, campus ministries, youth fellowships, Christian literature, evangelism, and world mission. Each of these functional arms reaches into a comparable committee in most well-organized state societies, and the major metropolitan and area organizations throughout the nation. The huge body of paid and voluntary personnel involved in the United Christian Missionary Society machine determines to a great degree the actions of the subsidiary and related organizations of the churches. In fact, the women's auxiliary of the UCMS, known as the Christian Women's Fellowship, will probably be the chief factor in assuring the achievement of Restructure.

The device of Unified Promotion, which is in control of almost all fiscal phases of the organizational life of the Brotherhood, is a vital factor in forcing Restructure. Congregations and agencies are being compelled to entrust every area of their Christian stewardship to this body. It has closed the door to individual and independent initiative in either raising or expending funds. "Faithful stewardship" is now defined as giving only to headquarters-approved and -controlled objectives and concerns. It is believed by many competent observers that Unified Promotion may become the medium through which legal claim will be laid to many local churches, compelling their identification with the new denomination.

A word should be said about the colleges and seminaries affiliated with the Board of Higher Education. They were advised in an executive session of officers and board members of the national agencies held in Detroit, October 7, 1964, that a responsible national board would be set up under Restructure which would determine whether these schools would continue to operate as at present, be merged with other schools or be reorganized to meet new needs. This board would also have the power to determine whether sources of support would be reapportioned and whether new schools could be organized.

(5) *International Convention.* At the Detroit Assembly, Report 34 proposed[15] changes which would transform the International Convention of Christian Churches (Disciples of Christ) into an official "delegate convention." The proposal, to be ratified at the Dallas Assembly in 1966, calls for a four-level controlled delegate system: (a) local congregations would be represented by three votes each for *approved* memberships up to 1,000, and one additional delegate for each 500 additional *approved* members; (b) the *principal* members of the Committee on Recommendations; (c) the *voting* members of the Council of Agencies; and (d) the officers and staff members of the Convention itself. Resolution 30 (at Detroit) provided for a Convention Credentials Committee which would have final authority to seat delegates. Resolution 47 provided a new definition of *active* or *approved* members of local congregations. It eliminates all brethren who are not wholeheartedly in favor of all local, area and national policies approved by Indianapolis, from consideration for appointment as official delegates to state, area or national conventions. Thus a controlled Assembly at Dallas will approve these new proposals, constitute itself the official voice of the Brotherhood and vote full approval of Restructure. The new Assembly is to meet only every other year and between meetings a General Council of 200 to 300 members would meet as a deliberative body. A smaller Executive Board, elected by the General Council, would meet three times a year to actually direct the affairs of the Brotherhood.

(6) *Ecumenical Relationships.* Restructure of the Brotherhood is not an end in itself. It is a means by which a hitherto loosely-associated community of Free Churches may be transformed into a legally constituted centrally controlled denomination and delivered by means of mergers into one united ecumenical Church. The Establishment is now participating in the current Consultation on Church Union[17] and has already committed itself to many grave compromises of our dis-

tinctive testimony to the Christian world. The final chapter of our study is devoted to this development and its meaning to our Free Churches.

Before it is everlastingly too late, those who still claim allegiance to the Christ and to the Church of the New Testament need to take a firm stand against Restructure. We like the word of warning (taken somewhat out of context but containing broad implications) given by Dr. Garrison in his Kansas City address: "As the nature of the end must always determine the nature of the means to be employed for its attainment, so it is essential that we should not build into our program for immediate denominational aggrandizement any elements that are inconsistent with the wider unity for which we work and pray. If the history of Christianity proves anything at all, it proves that the church cannot be united on a basis of either a 'large measure of agreement in doctrine' (to quote the exact words of Dr. W. A. Visser 't Hooft) or a uniform system of polity which will bring the whole church under one administrative organizational structure. I am not only convinced by the study of history that this is true, but I am glad that it is true, for I am equally convinced that any such theological and institutional solidification would be disastrous . . ."

Chapter XII

THE NEW CATHOLICISM

R ESTRUCTURE is being proposed at a time when most of Christendom is deeply concerned about its divisions and is engaged in a massive drive toward the achievement of One Great Church.[1] Restructure is being advocated as essential to the realization of this goal. This is good ecclesiastical strategy. It enables the Establishment to brand all opposition to Restructure as divisive and opposed to the unity of all the followers of Christ.

The Restoration Movement, as we have made clear in previous chapters, seeks to promote Christian unity. It presents a practical plan for its accomplishment: a return to the Bible and the Bible alone as the rule of faith and practice and a restoration of the New Testament Church in doctrine, ordinances and life. The means thus proposed remains the most feasible and, above all, the most Scriptural thus far advanced. Union by compromise, merger or absorption might bring about a united Church, but it would bear no resemblance to the Church which Jesus built and would inevitably degenerate into a Catholicism similar to that which arose in the third century and eventuated into the ecclesiastical tyranny of Rome.

Advocates of Restructure have rejected the Restoration principle and with it the Free Church idea.[2] They say that "the theory of unqualified congregational independence and autonomy is incompatible with the ecumenical ideal . . . and cannot be carried as a theory of unity into the ecumenical church." At the same time they seek to placate the friends of freedom by asserting that none of the Christian values that belong to the Free Churches will be sacrificed by the achievement of One Church for One World. Indeed, they say, they would be enhanced by an ecumenical fellowship with other Christians.

Members of the Establishment have been moving, with the tacit approval of the International Convention and without waiting for the confirmation of their Restructure program, to prepare the way for the next logical step which will be "Merger" with other denominations. The first official move toward Merger was taken by the Convention in 1946 when it adopted resolutions advocating the idea. In 1949 at Greenwich, Connecticut, the Establishment participated in the first attempt of friendly denominations to draft a blueprint for a united church. Thereafter, ICCC resolutions were burdened with proposals to unite with the Congregationalists, and, after 1957, with the United Church of Christ. Then, in 1960, Dr. Eugene Carson Blake, stated clerk of the United Presbyterian Church in the USA, proposed in his historic sermon in Grace Episcopal Cathedral in San Francisco, that the Presbyterians, Episcopalians and Methodists unite. At the first meeting (April, 1962), of the Consultation which grew out of the Blake proposal, the Disciples of Christ were invited to become full participants in this union endeavor. With International Convention approval,[3] they, with the United Church of Christ and the Evangelical United Brethren, have constituted a six-church group[4] which in the spring of 1963 outlined a possible plan of organic union.[5] When this rough draft has been properly phrased and polished, it will be presented for consideration by the official denominational bodies involved. Everything appears to be moving "according to plan."

Disciples' representatives in the Consultation have tentatively agreed to all sorts of compromises. They have indicated that they would accept a strong centralized Super-Church authority which would enable the related churches to act unitedly and effectively in socio-political concerns. They have assented to the necessity of a covenant or creedal statement as a mutual expression of faith and practice. They have intimated that all varieties of baptismal practice now existent in the participating denominations would be recognized as adequate, thus validating the "open membership" policy long advocated by the Establishment. They look with favor upon making the Lord's Supper more meaningful by accenting its liturgical and sacramental significance and requiring that it be observed only under the supervision of an ordained ministry. They have accepted the Catholic doctrine of Apostolic Succession and ordination of ministers by bishops as essential to the perpetuation of an authentic ministry. They have agreed to abandon the Restoration principle as essential to true Christian Unity and the Free Church polity as relevant to modern Church structure. While all these commitments are at this stage purely tentative and subject to official approval by the new Restructured Christian Church there is little doubt but that they have the full endorsement of the Establishment.

But this is not the end of the dream. The next step beyond Merger will be "Ecumenical Amalgamation" and the realization of a "Disappearing Brotherhood." Leaders of the Establishment have long insisted that in harmony with its goal of a United Church the Restoration Movement must inevitably be lost in a resulting Catholic or Universal Church. The blueprint for this achievement is well advanced. The International Convention for years has been passing resolutions approving the active participation of Disciples of Christ in the work of the World Council of Churches. Its official representatives have occupied seats of high honor in WCC conclaves, commissions and committees. The Council has repeatedly denied that it is a Super-Church or that it will be the "Coming Great Church" which it so strongly advocates. Yet within its framework (largely in the Commission on Faith and Order) all the major consultations on Christian unity at the world level are taking place.[6] The latest available count of negotiations lists 38 separate talks, involving 102 denominations in 30 countries. Among them are plans for union of the General Synod of the Anglican Church of Canada and the United Church of Canada; the British Methodist Union and the Church of England; a "summit conference" involving the Church of England, the Presbyterian Church of England, the Church of Scotland (Presbyterian), and the Episcopal Church of Scotland; Anglicans, Brethren, Disciples, Methodists, Baptists, Presbyterians and Congregationalists in North India and Pakistan; Presbyterians, Methodists, Congregationalists, Anglicans and Disciples in New Zealand; in Australia — Anglicans, Methodists, Presbyterians and Disciples; "united churches" are being created in Zambia, Nigeria, East Africa, Ghana, Malagasy and Cameroon. The Establishment is doing its best to persuade leaders in our British, Australian and New Zealand Churches of Christ to enter the new associations and mergers under consideration in their countries.

And even this is not all. The World Council of Churches is engaged in the encouragement of rapprochement with the Roman Catholic Church. Its concern about the eventual union of the Eastern Orthodox (Greek) Catholic Church and the Roman Church is beginning to show results. There are serious overtures being made to the Jewish world community and other non-Christian religious faiths. In the prophetic words of Dr. Edwin T. Dahlberg at the 1958 Saint Louis Assembly of the International Convention, "The ecumenical movement will undoubtedly go beyond the borders of the Christian religion in its desire to bring all religions into one great united family of God." All the churches which approve Restructure will eventually be officially involved in active participation in the sweeping movement for the achievement of this World Church which cannot possibly approximate in any way the Church that Jesus built.

We might well raise the question as to whether this high-handed series of official actions of the International Convention approving this headlong plunge into such a questionable melange of ecumenical adventures is legal. The Convention has never in its history (until now) claimed to be more than a voluntary association of such churches and individuals as may have desired its services. The churches listed in its *Year Book* have never been polled to see whether they approved or disapproved the Convention's right and power to turn the long-standing fellowship of Free Churches into a national unitary or corporate church. If it has the powers it now claims, they were never conferred by the local churches. If the Establishment which controls the Convention is responsible for these patently illegal claims and has thus ruthlessly ignored the rights of the local churches, how can these churches trust its leadership in forming Restructured organizations at area, regional, national or international levels? Why do they insist on avoiding a comprehensive plebiscite of all the churches? If the strategies the Establishment has employed in the past to achieve their purposes are any indication of their tactics in the future, what is to hinder their delivery into alien control the whole complex of agencies and conventions we have built up through past decades of our history together with the large funds they have acquired? Of course, it is now claimed that with the advent of a "delegate convention" the problem of legal authority will be solved. But what about the thousands of local congregations that will not have committed themselves on the right of any Convention to represent them and that do not even recognize the right of the International Convention to poll the Free Churches?

The fact of the matter is, the Establishment has decreed that "Free Church polity must be destroyed." It knows that congregationalism, so long as truly held by the Brotherhood, and so long as protected by law, constitutes an insurmountable legal obstacle to the attainment of a unified corporate centrally-controlled denomination.

This antipathy for the Free Church has been well expressed by that high priest of the Establishment, Dr. Charles Clayton Morrison, distinguished founder and long-time editor of *The Christian Century*. In his history-making Beecher Lectures at Yale, he elaborated the thesis that congregationalism, the polity of the Free Churches, is the greatest obstacle to the attainment of the ecumenical goal. His vigorous indictment is contained in his books *What Is Christianity?* and *The Unfinished Reformation.* He says that congregationalism derives chiefly "from Protestant biblicism, and from an utterly unimaginative form of biblicism." Then seemingly on the basis of a philosophy which holds that only the material is real, he argues that for congregationalists the Church, existing only as an idea, has no reality and can have none even though a mystical veneration be given it. He brilliantly contends that congregationalism is the culmination of Protestant principles and other *passe* idealisms such as individualism, nationalism, capitalism, and democracy. To these idealisms he attributes the collapse of Western civilization and places Protestantism at the top of the list. He then calls upon Protestants and congregationalists to repudiate their outworn fetishes and their exhausted allies. All the time, he holds, we have available a better guide than the Bible and contends that Christianity should rely basically upon its own revelation — the best tradition of the historic Church. It should give its loyalty to a visible ecclesiasticism through which God can reveal His ever-evolving will perpetually relevant to the times in which men live.

Dr. Morrison thus espouses the cause of a New Catholicism. His argument is the ground of the Old Testament religious institutional views which led to the death of Jesus because He rejected them. It is of a psychological piece with divine imperialisms of many peoples. The Church as God's divine revelation, relying on its subsidiary and supporting revelations, and on its own judgment of itself and its powers, was the basic reason why, for cultural progress, the world has had to be periodically emancipated from religion, as a condition necessary for progress. If it is the Church that speaks God's word of truth for successive generations only through official interpreters, assembled councils, or an infallible pope, what of the purported revelations of Christ and the Apostles as recorded in the Bible? Would they be disregarded if they were in conflict with the edicts of these Living Oracles? No attacks by agnostics or infidels could be more damaging to Christendom than such a debasing of the standards of truth by its accredited champions. Dr. Morrison, in his labored argument, is really reverting to the hoary doctrines of the third century Catholics who believed that unity consists in privilege, order, succession, creed, and visible structure rather than in terms of spiritual commitment, insight, fellowship, and obedience to Christ in all things according to the Scriptures. His successors in the Disciples' Establishment are so committed to the philosophy of institutionalism that its advancement has become an obsession. They and their followers are unable to see beyond ecclesiastical institutions and agencies which have become for them the veritable warp and woof of the Church — the visible and sensible oneness and wholeness essential to felt unity. For them unity on the basis of habit, instinct, place learning and the physical senses is the only unity worth contending for.

Dr. Morrison's successors in the World Council of Churches speak the same language and are equally determined that "congregationalism must die." Colin Williams[7] was authorized by its Third Assembly at

New Delhi to prepare a document to be issued by the WCC Department of Studies in answer to the question, "Is the present form of church life a major hindrance to the work of evangelism?" Dr. Williams gives savage treatment to the local church. He concludes that if the Church is to be true to its mission, it must undergo drastic changes in its polity. The local church, he says, centering around the homes of its members and the work of the congregation led by an ordained minister must be scrapped as a means of meeting the world's needs. He calls such a concept "the myth of the local." He says people no longer live where they live and that the New Testament idea of "the church in the house" is irrelevant in a Space Age. He repeats Morrison by branding the idea of a resident congregation as "morphological fundamentalism" which still appeals to the Bible as authority for church polity. The words "structure" and "restructure" are frequently used in his book. He calls for Restructure of the Church around the needs of the world and insists that the time has come to abandon the idea that the Church is the custodian of the faith and proclaimer of the Gospel through which men may be saved and social change may be accomplished. This is a day for "dialogue between the Church and the World" with the World "writing the agenda." The New Testament, says Williams, must be reinterpreted in such a way as to make possible a thorough Restructure of the Church which will henceforth take its form in response to the structures of world need.[8]

Those who advocate the achievement of Restructure by a "reinterpretation" of the New Testament are really engaged in an immoral undertaking. They know that in order to achieve their ends they must convince a vast body of naive and trusting people who still love the Word of God and would not knowingly do anything opposed to its teaching, and that they must do it by a misuse of Scripture and the twisting of texts. This is exactly what the Church Fathers of the third century did to brainwash the Free Churches and achieve Catholicism. Dean Inge once said, "Powerful churchmen have often gained the upper hand by methods utterly opposed to the spirit of Christ. As Berdyaev says, men have set themselves apart to hate in the cause of love, to use compulsion in the name of freedom, and to become practicing materialists for the inculcation of spiritual principles." Disciples of Christ are now being flooded with literature that does exactly this to win the battle for Restructure. And the men who write and preach these heresies are the ones who ask for the full trust and commitment of the brethren in their leadership as they move into the next phases of Merger and Ecumenical Amalgamation.

The unity that is being promised as the result of Restructure, Merger and Ecumenical Amalgamation is not the unity for which Christ prayed (John 17). The only result of the studies, conferences, consultations, conventions, resolutions, covenants and legislative and judicial actions will be Ecclesiastical Monopoly, exactly the same thing that eventuated following the Apostasy of the third century. Monopolism, whether in business, government or religion easily becomes the instrument of tyranny. The totalitarian church is as much to be dreaded as the totalitarian state — possibly more because the monopolistic church wields its control over the hearts and consciences of men as well as over their social and political structures. Students of history cannot ignore the record of the Old Catholicism in era after era and in nation after nation, in which it became the symbol of oppression, exercising dominion over every phase of life and destroying human freedom. It might take centuries, but a New Catholicism, because of its very nature, would inevitably become like the Old.

This fear of eventual identification of the modern Ecumenical movement with Roman Catholicism is not a creature of our imagination. Probably the most dramatic evidence of this new rapprochement was the visit of Geoffrey Fisher,[9] then primate of the Church of England and a president of the World Council of Churches, to the Pope on the afternoon of December 3, 1960. Two days before, Dr. Fisher preached a sermon justifying his visit (the first from an English archbishop in 400 years), in All Saint's Anglican cathedral in Rome. Pastors and leaders representing denominations in the Federal Council of Churches of Italy had been invited to hear the historic apologetic. He paid high tribute to "what the Roman Church has done for us all in its strength and authority." He expressed regret for "the bitter strife not yet healed between the conception of an imperial Church and the more ancient conception of a commonwealth of Churches within the Church of Christ." He said his visit was for the purpose of promoting universal Christian unity and that the phase of ecumenicity now being entered is of unique significance and calls for mature thought and daring adventure. Dr. Fisher elaborated on his "commonwealth" idea of a polity for the Coming Great Church (reminiscent of the British Commonwealth of nations bound together by common ties to the royal head), in which the major streams of Christendom can exist in peace, cease to be competitive and become co-operative and powerfully influential. The clear intimation of Dr. Fisher was that the Pope might well be eventually accepted as the unifying Head of One Church for One World. Since that day in Rome the World Council and the Roman Church have each set up official agencies of communication, and dialogue is beginning to take place at every level of church life throughout the world looking toward first, better understanding, and, then, eventual unity.

The true unity of the Church derives, not from a centralized authoritative ecclesiastical structure, but from real spiritual substance. It is not, as we have previously indicated, something that can be achieved by voting it or desiring it. It is more than a sentimental "togetherness"; more than a sanctified camaraderie; more than fellowship in a coffee hour or a coffee house; more than worship in a common liturgy; more than association under a common name; more than participation in a common program issued from a central headquarters; more than a common mood or an attitude; more than a mere outflowing of goodwill. The true unity has its roots in common loyalty to Jesus Christ, the only true Head of the Church; in a common acceptance of the truth revealed in the Word of God, and in a mutual purpose implicit in the Gospel.

The true freedom in the Church is to be found where the true unity obtains. This freedom, as we have discovered previously in our study, begins with freedom in Christ which we know as a result of our complete commitment to Him, and expresses itself in the service of truth and love to all mankind. As Brunner puts it:[10] "Only he is free who is reconciled with God, with himself and with his fellows; only he is free who is utterly dependent upon God; and whosoever is 'free indeed,' through the Son who makes him dependent upon the Father, is entirely committed and entirely bound up with the life of his fellows."

What is called the Church in history — the institutional *Ecclesia* — permits men but little of this freedom. It interposes itself between the individual and God to such a degree that the life in Christ described in the Holy Scriptures cannot be fully realized. This is why so many people are disillusioned about the Church, becoming either formal and lukewarm in their attitude, or refusing altogether to have anything to do with it. The proposed merger of many denominations into an institutional behemoth will not solve this problem. Indeed, it may be the means of further misleading Christians into identifying the true Church with the institution, and even the living Christ with the institution. It is pre-eminently in the Free Churches, unalloyed by superfluous institutionalism and hierarchal domination that the Holy Spirit of God will be able freely and powerfully to work according to God's Word to restore the Church in all its pristine power and glory.

Brunner envisions[11] the dangers of an Ecumenical Church which depends upon institutional structure for its unity. He warns "(The institutional church) has again and again stood revealed as one of the major obstacles to the creation and the preservation of the pure *Ecclesia,* and particularly so, when it has boasted of being identical with the whole Christian community, and has named Christ and the Church in the same breath." The current popular movement toward a New Catholicism could well eventuate in a Christianity which will again betray Christ, as did the Old Catholicism, in the interest of "the unity of all Christians."

We believe that the unity of all God's people may some day be fully attained by the sincere application of the principles revealed in the New Testament and so winsomely portrayed in the *Declaration and Address* by Thomas Campbell. This is no dream. Some of our greatest Biblical theologians are beginning to think in these terms. Karl Barth's view of the Church universal[12] coincides in many respects with the historic position of the Disciples. In his small volume, *The Church and the Churches,* he frequently refers to New Testament passages, to emphasize his conviction that the Church must be united "in the One, in Jesus Christ as the one Son of God, the bestower of the one Holy Spirit." Its basis lies in God's grace and in no secondary principle distinguishable from grace. He urges that the quest for the

one Church must be "concerned with the imperative content of the
acknowledgment that there is one Lord, one faith, one baptism, one
God above all, for all and in all . . . The quest for the unity of the
Church must in fact be identical with the quest for Jesus Christ as the
concrete Head and Lord of the Church. The blessing of unity cannot
be separated from Him who blesses, for in Him it has its source and
reality, through His Word and Spirit it is revealed to us, and only
through faith in Him can it become a reality among us." Barth makes
it clear in his treatise that mere union in a federation or council of
churches is not true Christian unity. Such a union would be merely
"something which the Church would have in common with human
societies and undertakings in general . . . A mere federation in itself
has nothing at all to do with real Church union."

Barth expresses sympathy for all ecumenical movements but points
out that their efforts will be futile if they eventuate in nothing more
than "mutual tolerance, respect, and co-operation; readiness to hear
and understand one another; an emotional sense of oneness in the
possession of some ineffable common link, or, more than that, worshipping together in one accord." Above all, says Barth, the "decisive
test of unity is joining in making our confession of faith and unitedly
proclaiming it to the world, thus fulfilling the commandment of Jesus
on which the Church is based. The message and witness, given by the
Church's teaching, order and life, must utter one voice, however mani-
fold in the diversity of languages, gifts, of place and persons. A union
of the churches in the sense that the task which is so seriously laid
upon the Church would mean a union of all confessions in the one
unanimous Confession." To arrive at this united testimony, Barth says
in his closing appeal that the mere syllogistic approach based on human
presuppositions is inadequate and will fall short of achieving the ultimate end. "We must listen to Christ, *The Christ of the Scriptures*,
for the answer."

Christian unity consists in that which may be quite simply stated,
that is, a faith expressed in accordance with the mind of Christ as
exhibited in the writings of the New Testament and *in nothing else.*

YE SHALL KNOW THE TRUTH AND THE TRUTH
SHALL SET YOU FREE — John 8:32

A PRAYER FOR UNITY

GRACIOUS God, our Heavenly Father, we thank Thee for the
Church of Jesus Christ. We thank Thee that Thou didst so love
us as to send Thine only begotten Son into the world to give His life
a ransom for all men who believe upon His Name.

We thank Thee, our God, that we have been purchased by His
precious atoning blood, born again and made a part of His glorious
body the Church. We thank Thee for the blessed fellowship we know
in Thee through Thy dear Son — one flock, one fold and one Shepherd.
We find in Jesus Christ our life, our hope, our all.

We thank Thee for Thy Holy Word and the Holy Spirit whereby
we are grounded, upheld and guided and preserved in Holy Communion
with Thee.

As we look upon the outward divisions of the Church in the world
our hearts are pained. God forgive our humanisms, our perversities
and our feverish ways which promote divisions, which keep us from
fellowship one with another and which hinder the evangelization of
the world. We long for the visible realization of the unity for which
Christ prayed. We would surrender our will completely to Thee that
Thy will may be done in us to the unity of Thy people and to Thy
everlasting glory.

We pray Thy divine blessing upon all those movements and
agencies which seek in sincerity the true and ultimate unity of Thy

people in the earth. Guide them in Thy Truth to do Thy will. Bless especially, we beseech Thee, those earnest souls who have dedicated their lives to the achievement of this holy purpose. Keep them in Thy will and way. Deliver them from presumptuous thoughts, precipitous acts and shameful compromises.

Hinder and destroy, we beseech Thee, every device of men or of Satan which would mar the pattern of the Church which Jesus built and which His chosen Apostles have revealed to us in Thy Holy Word.

Forbid, O God, that unity which would compromise Thy eternal Truth, condone evil, dampen our zeal for lost souls, consent to barren profession, bear no spiritual fruit, take pride in outward show, seek political power and number in its company a people who praise Thee with their lips but whose hearts are far from Thee. Fulfill the heartening promise of our Lord that the gates of hell shall not prevail against Thy Church.

Help us to know the mind of Christ and His will for us in all things pertaining to His Church, that in His greatness we may rise above our littleness, in His strength we shall lose our weakness, in His peace we may bury all discord that in His truth and righteousness we may march — the united Church militant accomplishing the work Thou hast set for us in our day and time.

At last, we pray, enfold us in the one Church triumphant, the family of God, to dwell with Thee forever. And unto Thee we will ascribe all honor and glory through Jesus Christ, our Lord. Amen.

NOTES AND REFERENCES

AUTHOR'S PREFACE

[1] Loren E. Lair's *The Christian Churches and Their Work* deals with related subjects but is in no sense a definitive work on congregational church polity.

[2] Dated September 1, 1965.

CHAPTER I

[1] Caine, *op. cit.*, p. 345.

[2] The terms *freedom* and *liberty* are used interchangeably in this volume. Freedom is usually obtained "for" or "from" something and indicates an absence of external restraint. Liberty has a strong individual flavor and is a condition of the mind rather than the body. Thus Byron could properly speak of the prisoner of Chillon as having liberty while chained in a dungeon. It has been said that liberty exists in proportion to wholesome restraint. This element of self-control has spiritual and ethical overtones and is found in the words of the Apostle Paul, "Where the Spirit of the Lord is, there is liberty." Thus, liberty might be said to be something more elevated than the condition of mundane freedom. Since, however, the dictionary seems to sanction interchangeable use of the two words, we will follow that accepted practice.

[3] Fairbairn, *op. cit.*, p. 89.

[4] Fairbairn, *op. cit.*, pp. 12, 13.

[5] Hayden, *Church Polity*, pp. 32, 33.

CHAPTER II

[1] *Cf.*, Brunner, *The Misunderstanding of the Church*, p. 12.

[2] Quoted by Hayden, *Church Polity*, pp. 16, 17ff.

[3] Ernest F. Scott, *The Nature of the Early Church*.

[4] Hayden, *op. cit.*, p. 33.

[5] *The Misunderstanding of the Church*, p. 33.

[6] Philo Judaeus, *The Works of Philo Judaeus* (tr. Yonge).

[7] *Genesis of the New England Churches*, chapter on "Christian Church Polity," p. 17.

[8] *Ibid*, p. 18.

[9] *Declaration and Address*, Proposition Three.

[10] Johann Lorenz von Morsheim, *Institutes of Ecclesiastical History Ancient and Modern* (tr. Murdock), pp. 60-78.

CHAPTER III

[1] As translated by Alexander Roberts, *The Ante-Nicene Fathers.*

[2] Salutation, *Epistle of Clement to the Church at Corinth.*

[3] *Ibid.,* c. 34.

[4] *Ibid.,* c. 54.

[5] *Ibid.,* c. 57.

[6] *Ibid.,* c. 54.

[7] *Ibid.,* c. 44.

[8] *Epistle of Polycarp to the Church at Philippi,* c. 3.

[9] *Ibid.,* c. 6.

[10] Many regard the epistles of Ignatius as spurious. See Gibbon's *Decline and Fall of the Roman Empire,* Vol. I, Ch. 15, note 70.

[11] Of somewhat doubtful authority, though very ancient.

[12] *Epistle of Hermas,* c. 2 and 4.

[13] *Epistle of Cyprian,* Ep. LXXVIII, p. 117.

[14] *Op. cit.,* Ep. V, p. 11.

[15] *Cf.,* Emil Brunner, *The Misunderstanding of the Church,* Ch. III.

[16] *Cf.,* Liston Pope, *Millhands and Preachers,* pp. 122-124.

[17] The historical developments cited in this chapter are verifiable in all major histories of the Christian Church. See Bibliography.

[18] *A Catechism of Christian Doctrine, No. 3,* official revised edition of *The Baltimore Catechism,* issued by the Roman Catholic Confraternity of Christian Doctrine.

CHAPTER IV

[1] Broadbent, *op. cit.,* p. 35.

[2] *Ibid.,* p. 36.

[3] W. S. Gilly, *Vigilantius and His Times.*

[4] Gunnar Westin, *The Free Church Through the Ages,* pp. 12-15.

[5] *Ibid.,* pp. 9-12.

[6] LeRoy Edwin Froom, *The Prophetic Faith of Our Fathers,* Vol. I, pp. 816-818. *Cf.,* Peter Alix, *Ecclesiastical History of Piedmont,* Ch. IX.

[7] Froom, *ibid.,* pp. 824-826.

[8] *Ibid.,* Ch. XXXIV.

[9] Gunnar Westin, *The Free Church Through the Ages,* pp. 27-30.

[10] Froom, *op. cit.,* chart and tabulated sources, pp. 944-952.

[11] Jacques-Benigne Bossuet, *The History of the Variations of the Protestant Churches,* Vol. II.

[12] Charles Beard, *The Reformation of the Sixteenth Century,* p. 25ff.

[13] E. H. Broadbent, *The Pilgrim Church,* pp. 117-123.

[14] Gunnar Westin, *The Free Church Through the Ages,* pp. 30-35.

[15] *Ibid.,* pp. 35-37.

[16] P. G. Mode, *Dictionary of Religion and Ethics,* p. 225.

[17] E. H. Broadbent, *The Pilgrim Church,* pp. 141-149.

[18] *Ibid.*, Ch. IX.

[19] W. B. Selbie, *Congregationalism*, Ch. II.

[20] An entire volume might be written concerning the development of the Free Church movement in Great Britain since the eighteenth century. The vigor of Free Church life there is a tremendous testimony to its contention that the Church when tied to government or to a prevailing cultural pattern is not at liberty to be the Church which was founded by Jesus Christ.

[21] Selbie, *ibid.*, Ch. V.

[22] Alexander Haldane, *Memoirs of R. and J. A. Haldane.*

[23] Richardson, *op. cit.*, Vol. I, Chs. X and XI.

CHAPTER V

[1] Churches of Christ (non-instrument), 2,300,000; Christian Churches and Churches of Christ (co-operative and independent), 2,000,000; overseas churches and missions of all groups, 1,000,000.

[2] James DeForest Murch, *Christians Only*, pp. 19-122.

[3] Robert Richardson, *Memoirs of Alexander Campbell* (see index under Thomas Campbell).

[4] Campbell, *op cit.* (Centennial Edition), pp. 6, 16, 17.

[5] Robert Richardson, *Memoirs of Alexander Campbell*, discussion of formative influences, Vol. I, pp. 166-190.

[6] *Ibid.*, Vol. I, pp. 365-368, 403, 430.

[7] Henry K. Shaw, *Buckeye Disciples*, pp. 55-59.

[8] C. C. Ware, *Barton Warren Stone* (*cf.*, William G. West, *Barton Warren Stone*).

[9] *Ibid.*, Ch. X.

[10] W. T. Moore, *Comprehensive History of the Disciples of Christ*, pp. 243-246.

[11] James DeForest Murch, *Christians Only*, Ch. VII.

CHAPTER VI

[1] Alexander Campbell used this expression to denote the First Dispensation of God's grace. In his famous "Sermon on the Law" he called the Second Dispensation "The Moonlight Age," and the Third, "The Sunlight Age." They are now commonly designated, The Patriarchal, The Jewish, and The Christian dispensations.

[2] Alfred Edersheim, *Life and Times of Jesus the Messiah*, 5th Ed., Vol. I, pp. 431-450.

[3] Monroe, *op. cit.*, pp. 230, 231.

[4] Whyte, *op. cit.*, pp. 3-59, 365-381.

CHAPTER VII

[1] Hayden, *op. cit.*, pp. 9-18.

[2] For a more complete legal history of free church polity among the Christian Churches and Churches of Christ see *The Legal Implications of Church Structure*, by Attorney Luther D. Burrus.

CHAPTER VIII

[1] Campbell, *op. cit.*, Vol. I., pp. 20,28,49,51,54,59,71,103,105.

[2] Quoted in *Christian Ministers Manual*, James DeForest Murch, ed.

[3] The Raines incident, which called forth the quoted comments of Thomas and

Alexander Campbell is treated *in extenso* by W. T. Moore in his *Comprehensive History of the Disciples of Christ*, pp. 286-296.
4 Briney, in *Watchword of the Restoration Vindicated*, p. 30.
5 Included in *The Direction of Brotherhood Restructure*, pp. 21-27.

CHAPTER IX

1 Among the hundreds of citations which might be assembled to prove this assertion, none is more trenchant and convincing than Alexander Campbell's "Lunenburg Letter" and attendant comments. The "Letter" appeared in the *Millennial Harbinger* for September, 1837, and his further comments in the November and December issues of the same year.
2 Hayden, *op. cit.*, pp. 140,141.
3 Milligan, *op. cit.*, p. 407.
4 Campbell, *op. cit.*, March 1850.
5 Errett, *op. cit.*
6 Corey, *Fifty Years of Attack and Controversy*, p. 278.
7 Hayden, *op. cit.*, p. 165.
8 *Ibid.*, p. 166.
9 *Ibid.*, pp. 166, 167.
10 *Ibid.*, pp. 168, 171.
11 Ibid., pp. 171,172,175,176.
12 Spinka, *op. cit.*, p. 79.
13 In "Revolution and Religion," *This Week* magazine, December 26, 1965.

CHAPTER X

1 For a more extensive treatment see the author's work, *Christians Only*, Chapter XII, "The Rise of Conventions and Agencies."
2 *Cf.*, Charles Louis Loos, *Our First General Convention*.
3 *Cf.*, Henry K. Shaw, *Buckeye Disciples*, pp. 169-176.
4 *Centennial Convention Report.*
5 Earl Irvin West, *Search for the Ancient Order*, Vol. I, pp. 428-448.
6 Lair, *op. cit.*, p. 122.
7 Garrison and DeGroot, *op. cit.*, pp. 381,382.
8 The term *Establishment*, in its religious connotations, had its origin in England. There the State or Established Church was known to be politically controlled and motivated. As a result, the common people dubbed the combined Church-State authority "The Establishment."
9 This paper was entitled, "Analysis of the Participating Communions" and was a sociologically oriented report prepared at the request of the Consultation. The Disciples denomination was officially represented at Oberlin.
10 *Cf.*, Loren E. Lair, *The Christian Churches and Their Work*, p. 160.
11 *Ibid.*, pp. 160,174-197, 246-261, 283-292.
12 *Ibid.*, p. 133.
13 The developments here recorded may be verified by a study of the actions of the International Convention and the reports of the agencies contained in the *Year Books* of the Convention from 1917 to the present time.

CHAPTER XI

[1] Excerpt from an address, "The Short Look and the Long Look — the Ecumenical Paradox."

[2] 1960 *Year Book*, pp. 25-31.

[3] *Louisville Times*, issue October 26, 1960.

[4] *The Direction of Brotherhood Restructure*, p. 7.

[5] 1964 *Year Book*, pp. 34-38.

[6] *The Christian*, issue February 2, 1965, p. 13.

[7] 1964 *Year Book*, pp. 38-40.

[8] *The Direction of Brotherhood Restructure*, p. 7. *Cf.*, pp. 5-20.

[9] 1964 *Year Book*, pp. 27-32, 38-40, 42,52,57,59,60.

[10] For example, "Constitution and Bylaws," First Christian Church, Reseda, California.

[11] *The Direction of Brotherhood Restructure*, pp. 21-27.

[12] *Where Thought and Action Meet*, the Workbook of the 1965 Assembly (San Bernardino), Christian Churches of Southern California. Also selected work papers. *Cf.*, *Restructive Report*, September, 1965, "Restructure in California," pp. 1, 2.

[13] *The Direction of Brotherhood Restructure*, pp. 12-15.

[14] *Restructure Report*, September, 1965, p. 2.

[15] 1964 *Year Book*, pp. 40-42.

[16] *The Direction of Brotherhood Restructure*, pp. 14, 15.

[17] *Where We Are in Church Union Conversations*, a report issued by the Council on Christian Unity.

CHAPTER XII

[1] John Knox, *The Early Church and the Coming Great Church*. Also, the author's critique of the World Council of Churches under the same title.

[2] Ronald E. Osborn, *Toward the Christian Church*, pp. 39-56.

[3] *Where We Are in Church Union Conversations*, p. 12.

[4] *Ibid.*, pp. 10,11.

[5] *Ibid.*, pp. 14-16.

[6] *Inter-Church News* (publication of the National Council of Churches in the U.S.A.), issue of October, 1965, p. 3.

[7] Colin Williams, executive director, Central Department of Evangelism, National Council of Churches, and chairman, Department of Studies in Evangelism, World Council of Churches.

[8] Williams, *Where in the World*, issued by the World Council of Churches.

[9] From dispatch to the American press by William C. Standridge, Jr., dated Rome, December 3, 1960.

[10] *The Misunderstanding of the Church*, p. 114.

[11] *Ibid.*, p. 117.

[12] Barth, *op. cit.*, pp. 24,25,27,59,60,66,67,89.

BIBLIOGRAPHY

ABBOTT, B. A., The Disciples: An Interpretation
AINSLEE, PETER, The Message of the Disciples for the Union of the Church
AINSLEE, PETER, Toward Christian Unity
ATKINS, GAIUS GLENN, History of American Congregationalism

BACON, LEONARD, Genesis of the New England Churches
BANOWSKY, WILLIAM S., The Mirror of a Movement
BARTH, KARL, The Church and the Churches
BATES, M. SEARLE, Religious Liberty: An Inquiry
BAXTER, WILLIAM, Life of Elder Walter Scott
BENDER, HAROLD S., Mennonite Origins in Europe
BLAKEMORE, WILLIAM BARNETT (Ed.), The Revival of the Churches
BRADSHAW, MARION JOHN, Free Churches and Christian Unity
BRIDENBAUGH, CARL, Mitre and Sceptre
BROADBENT, E. H., The Pilgrim Church
BROWN, WILLIAM ADAMS, Toward a United Church
BRUNNER, EMIL, The Misunderstanding of the Church

CAMPBELL, ALEXANDER, The Christian System
CAMPBELL, THOMAS, Declaration and Address
CAINE, HALL, The Life of Christ
CHELTSCHIZKI, PETER, The Net of Faith
CLARK, HENRY W., History of English Nonconformity
COMBA, EMILIO, History of the Waldenses
CONYBEARE, FRED C. (Tr.), The Key of Faith
COOKE, LESLIE E. (et al), The Fourth Freedom
COREY, STEPHEN J., Fifty Years of Attack and Controversy
CRAIG, CLARENCE TUCKER, The One Church in the Light of the New Testament

D'AUBIGNES, J. H. MERLE, History of the Reformation (Vol. I)
DAVIS, M. M., Restoration Movement of the Nineteenth Century
DEBLOIS, AUSTEN KENNEDY, The Church of Today and Tomorrow
DEGROOT, A. T., The Restoration Principle
DEMONTESQUIEU, BARON LA BREDE ET, The Republicanism of Christianity
DEXTER, HENRY MARTYN, Congregationalism as Seen in Literature

EDERSHEIM, ALFRED, The Life and Times of Jesus the Messiah
ENGLAND, STEPHEN J., We Disciples
ESCOTT, HARRY, A History of Scottish Congregationalism

FROOM, EDWIN LEROY, The Prophetic Faith of Our Fathers (Vol. I)

GARRISON, W. E. and DEGROOT, A. T., The Disciples of Christ: A History
GREEN, F. M., Christian Missions and Historical Sketches

HALL, EDWIN, The Puritans and Their Principles
HARNACK, ADOLF, The Mission and Expansion of Christianity
HARNACK, ADOLF, What is Christianity?
HAYDEN, EDWIN V., Fifty Years of Digression and Disturbance
HAYDEN, W. L., Church Polity
HERSHBERGER, GUY F., The Recovery of the Anabaptist Vision
HERTZMANN, HANS, The Beginnings of the Christian Church
HORTON, DOUGLAS, Congregationalism
HORTON, WALTER MARSHALL, Toward a Reborn Church

INGE, W. R., Mysticism and Religion

JORDAN, W. L., The Development of Religious Toleration in England

KERSHNER, FREDERICK D., How to Promote Christian Union
KILLEN, W. D., The Ancient Church
KNOX, JOHN, The Early Church and the Coming Great Church
KUROSAKI, KOKICHI, One Body in Christ

LAIR, LOREN E., The Christian Churches and Their Work
LATOURETTE, KENNETH S., A History of Christianity
LEWIS, EDWIN, The Biblical Faith and Christian Freedom
LEWIS, GRANT K., The American Christian Missionary Society
LITTELL, FRANKLIN HAMLIN, The Anabaptist View of the Church
LOISY, A. F., The Gospel and the Church
LOOS, CHARLES LOUIS, Our First General Convention

MACGREGOR, WILLIAM MALCOLM, Christian Freedom
MACPHERSON, ANDERSON, The Evolution of Congregationalism
MCGIFFERT, A. C., The Apostolic Age
MILLIGAN, ROBERT, The Scheme of Redemption
MILMAN, HENRY HART, The History of Christianity
MINEAR, PAUL S. (Ed.), The Nature of the Unity We Seek
MOFFATT, JAMES, The First Five Centuries
MONASTIER, ANTOINE, A History of the Vaudois Church
MOORE, W. T., Comprehensive History of the Disciples of Christ
MORRISON, CHARLES CLAYTON, The Unfinished Reformation
MORRISON, CHARLES CLAYTON, What Is Christianity?
MOSHEIM, JOHANN LORENZ VON, Institutes of Ecclesiastical History (Vol. I)
MURCH, JAMES DEFOREST, Christians Only
MURCH, JAMES DEFOREST, The Coming Great Church
MURCH, JAMES DEFOREST, The Growing Super Church

NEAL, DANIEL, History of the Puritans
NEANDER, AUGUSTUS, General History of the Christian Religion and Church
NUTTALL, GEOFFREY F., Visible Saints: The Congregational Way

OSBORN, RONALD E. (Ed.), The Reformation of Tradition
OSBORN, RONALD E., Toward The Christian Church
OSBORN, RONALD E., The Spirit of American Christianity

PAYNE, ERNEST A., The Anabaptists of the 16th Century and Their Influence on the Modern World
PAYNE, ERNEST A., The Fellowship of Believers
PEEL, ALBERT, The Savoy Declaration of Faith and Order
PFLEIDERER, OTTO, Primitive Christianity
PHILLIPS, THOMAS W., Church of Christ
PUNCHARD, JOHN, A View of Congregationalism

RAMSEY, W. M., The Church in the Roman Empire Before A.D. 170
RENAN, ERNEST, Les Origines du Christianisme
RICHARDSON, ROBERT, Memoirs of Alexander Campbell
ROBERTS, ALEXANDER (Tr.), The Ante Nicene Fathers
ROBERTSON, JAMES C., History of the Christian Church
ROBINSON, WILLIAM A., The Biblical Doctrine of the Church

SCHAFF, DAVID SCHLEY, History of the Christian Church
SCHAFF, PHILIP, History of the Christian Church
SCOTT, ERNEST F., The Nature of the Early Church
SELBIE, W. B., Congregationalism
SHAW, HENRY K., Buckeye Disciples
SPINKA, MATTHEW, The Quest for Church Unity

TOWNSEND, HENRY, The Claims of the Free Churches
TYLER, B. B., A History of the Disciples of Christ

VISSER 'T HOOFT, W. A., The Renewal of the Church

WADDINGTON, GEORGE, A History of the Church from the Earliest Ages to the Reformation
WALKER, W. R., The Ministering Ministry
WARE, C. C., Barton Warren Stone
WARREN, W. R. (Ed.), Survey of Service: Disciples of Christ
WEISS, JOHANNES, Earliest Christianity
WEST, EARL IRVIN, The Search for the Ancient Order
WEST, WILLIAM G., Barton Warren Stone
WESTIN, GUNNAR, The Free Church Through the Ages
WHITLEY, OLIVER READ, Trumpet Call of Reformation
WHYTE, WILLIAM J., JR., The Organization Man
WILBURN, RALPH G. (Ed.), The Reconstruction of Theology
WOODHOUSE, A. S. P. (Ed.), Puritanism and Liberty

Year Books of the Christian Churches (Disciples of Christ)

——————— Freedom or Restructure?

——————— The Truth About Restructure

——————— The Direction of Brotherhood Restructure

——————— Where We Are in Church Union Conversations

——————— What Brotherhood Co-operation Means